What Others are Saying About

PURE PRAISE FOR YOUTH

"There is a lot to love about this intense six-week bible study, but my favorite is how Dwayne has 'lowered the cookies' on a language shelf that's attainable for students while still 'raising the bar' in spiritual content to stretch them in their faith. A great balance that's rare to see in a youth devotional."

David Nasser • Author, pastor, and evangelist

"Dwayne Moore's exciting new book *Pure Praise for Youth* is not for the faint of heart, the posers, or those who are content to sit in the back row. This challenge is for those who desire to be 'all in,' full throttle and especially for those who have no desire to tap out in their walk with God. This generation seems to be addicted to that which is extreme and there's no way to live a high octane devotion to Jesus publicly except by having their private worship and praise as a priority. I've watched Dwayne Moore be involved in not only leading praise to several thousand, but also to be very involved in the prayer, the planning and the platform to calling this generation to true devotion."

Dr. Jay Strack • President and Founder, Student Leadership University
studentleadership.net

"The subject of worship is a familiar topic of discussion. But for many students it remains unfamiliar in their personal experience. Worship has been taught in such abstract ways that the core of worship as a life response is missed. In these timely, practical and doable sessions, Dwayne goes beneath the flowery lyrics and high rhetoric of worship to unearth the heart of worship in the lives of every student. The truth contained in these 6 sessions of *Pure Praise for Youth* will help students to know what it means to worship with understanding. To all the student pastors, Sunday school teachers and small group bible study leaders: Teach this material and watch *truth* transform your group into fully functional worshippers."

David Edwards • Speaker and author, Oklahoma City, Oklahoma

"I've never known a more authentic worshipper than Dwayne Moore Both onstage and offstage, his passion for Jesus is contagious. And I don't know anyone more qualified than Dwayne to write about lifestyle worship. *Pure Praise for Youth* will deepen students' love for Christ and fire up their desire to share him with the world."

Scott Dawson • Scott Dawson Evangelistic Association
StrengthToStand.com

S0-AHM-978

"In a world as technologically savvy as it is today, information is flying off the shelf at a speed like never before. With this, anyone can understand the difficulty in sifting through this mountain of data to get to the good stuff. As book after book is being written on the theory, ideology, and method of worship and worship leadership, it's not often that you will come across one that focuses its content around teens. So, youth pastor, parent, or friend: Pick up this book today if you know a young Christ follower that wants to know and understand worship, and ultimately Jesus, on a deeper level."

Kevin Huguley • Musician with Rush Of Fools
Worship Pastor of Christ City Church, Birmingham, Alabama

"For students, the lines have been blurred for what it truly means to praise God. Many have even made their own definitions. Dwayne Moore shows students in scripture that praising God is more than song or sermon, it is a life of surrender."

Matt Wilson • Executive Director, First Priority of Greater Birmingham

"Dwayne is calling today's generation of students to be fervently devoted to a live of worship. In this brilliant six-week Bible study, Dwayne encourages and challenges students with a passion that pours from the pages and ignites a fire in your soul. *Pure Praise for Youth* is a book that everyone must read."

Travis Ryan • Worship Leader, Saddleback Church, Integrity Music Artist

PURE PRAISE
FOR YOUTH

A Heart-Focused Study on Worship

DWAYNE MOORE

Foreword by Mark Hall of Casting Crowns

Group
Loveland, Colorado
group.com

Group resources actually work!

This Group resource incorporates our R.E.A.L. approach to ministry. It reinforces a growing friendship with Jesus, encourages long-term learning, and results in life transformation, because it's

Relational
Learner-to-learner interaction enhances learning and builds Christian friendships.

Experiential
What learners experience through discussion and action sticks with them up to 9 times longer than what they simply hear or read.

Applicable
The aim of Christian education is to equip learners to be both hearers and doers of God's Word.

Learner-based
Learners understand and retain more when the learning process takes into consideration how they learn best.

PURE PRAISE
FOR YOUTH

A Heart-Focused Study on Worship
DWAYNE MOORE

Visit our website: **group.com**

Credits

Editor: Carl Simmons	Cover Art Director: Paul Povolni
Chief Creative Officer: Joani Schultz	Book Designer: Jean Bruns
Executive Editor: Becki Manni	Print Production Artist: Joey Vining
Copy Editor: Bethany Schulenberg	Illustrator: Wes Comer/Frontlines Creative

All Scripture quotations, unless otherwise indicated, are taken from the Holy Bible, New International Version®, NIV®. Copyright © 1973, 1978, 1984 by Biblica, Inc.™ Used by permission of Zondervan. All rights reserved worldwide. www.zondervan.com

Library of Congress Cataloging-in-Publication Data
Pure praise for youth : a heart-focused study on worship / Dwayne Moore.
     p. cm.
  ISBN 978-0-7644-6657-1 (pbk. : alk. paper)
  1. Worship—Biblical teaching—Textbooks. 2. Bible. O.T. Chronicles, 2nd, XX—Textbooks. 3. Christian education—Textbooks for youth. I. Title.
  BS1345.6.L67M66 2011
  264.00835—dc22

                          2011012112

15 14 13 12 11 10   20 19 18 17 16

Printed in the United States of America.

C●NTENTS

FOREWORD

As a youth minister of a large youth group in Georgia and through my travels with Casting Crowns, I've met a ton of teenagers over the years. I used to wonder why I'd see some grow up in church, attend Christian events, maybe even have Christian moms and dads, and yet as soon as they were old enough to get jobs and own their own cars, they'd stop going to church. They would gradually lose interest in anything that had to do with Jesus.

What God began to show me over time was that the reason many of our students weren't walking with Jesus in college is that they never had a walk with Jesus in our student ministry—they had mine. They were borrowing my walk with Jesus. They were experiencing moments around the Savior, but not the Savior himself. You can have a great church, a great pastor, and even a great band, but you will begin to notice over time that none of these people are going home with you. When you get home, when you get to school, when you get to work, and when you get to Monday…it's just you and Jesus. You can't borrow someone else's walk with Jesus. You must have your own—or to put it another way, you can't just hang *around* the stream, so to speak; you have to actually *drink* from its incredible water.

You see, I can try all day to explain what the water from a mountain stream tastes like. I can use words like pure, natural, cold, clear, and invigorating. But the only people who really get what I'm saying—the only ones who understand just how good that water is—are the ones who've had a big cold drink of it themselves.

That's why I'm so excited about this book.

As you go through *Pure Praise for Youth*, Jesus—the *Living Water*—is going to meet you one-on-one. He wants you to experience his love, joy, and awesome refreshment in ways you never have before. This study will take you deep into the well of God's Word where you can get to know him better and worship him more freely and intimately.

Through what he's written in these pages, my friend Dwayne Moore will help you discover how to worship God and love on him everywhere and in everything you do. You're going to learn what "lifestyle worship" really means. You'll discover how to better discern when God is speaking to you. You'll get to know God's still, small voice. And those are just a few of the things God has in store for you in the weeks to come!

So as you dive into this worthwhile study, let me be the first to say: Welcome to the "watering hole"! Come get you a big cold drink of Living Water. Come thirsty, and leave completely satisfied with Jesus.

Mark Hall
Author, *Your Own Jesus*
Lead Singer, Casting Crowns

A CHALLENGE TO
GO EXTREME

Have you ever watched skydiving, skateboarding, or snowboarding—or maybe even done it? I remember being glued to my TV, watching the halfpipe competition at the 2010 Winter Olympics. Soaring through the crisp, clear, Canadian sky, snowboarders flew as high as 25 feet above the halfpipe at the top, doing spiraling, double-flipping moves high in the air. Amazingly, some of them landed and stayed on their feet the whole way down!

Athletes like these must push themselves to their limits, and beyond. They go to extreme measures to prepare their bodies to do things that are far above average and "normal." They endure hours of intense and grueling practice. Why? Because they love their sport and the satisfaction they get from being their best.

During the next six weeks, I'll be challenging you to "go extreme" in your worship of God. But it's not your body you'll push to the max. Instead, you'll stretch your spirit. If you accept this challenge, you'll condition your heart, mind, and soul in ways you might never have thought possible. And as a result, you'll have the privilege of knowing the God of the universe and worshipping him more intimately and powerfully than you ever imagined!

You might be thinking, So let's say I take you up on this "extreme worship" challenge; what will I have to *do*? Good question. For starters, you'll need to take at least 15 minutes a day to read and work through the daily devotions in this book. There are five devotions each week; this way, if you miss a day or two during the week, you can catch up on the weekend. Each devotion is filled with powerful truths and helpful ideas. You'll definitely need your Bible each day so you can look up Scriptures and meditate on them, and a pen to write down what God's showing you. You'll also commit a Bible verse to memory each week.

At the end of each devotional lesson are two sections: "Keep It Real" and "Keep It Pure." These are important times of reflection *and* action. You'll discover new and exciting ways to worship the Lord, and be challenged to try expressions of praise that might be beyond anything you've ever experienced. But don't fear! I promise you'll be more than glad you took a chance on these!

On the next page, you'll notice two identical forms called "I'm Going Extreme!" If you're serious about growing in your worship, I dare you to complete both these forms *now*. Be sure to tear out one and give it to your

PURE PRAISE
FOR YOUTH

friend, youth leader, pastor, parent, or someone who'll hold you accountable to complete this study. Keep the other one in this book to remind you of your commitment.

I strongly suggest finding a friend who'll do this study with you. This way you'll be able to talk about what you're discovering together, and encourage each other to stay faithful to following through with the daily lessons—and to what God's teaching each of you through them.

Better yet, do this study with a small group! We'll help. At the end of each week's readings is a weekly small-group session. Each session takes about an hour and includes questions and experiences that are fun, hard-hitting, or both. As your group digs in further and pushes each other forward together, your relationships with each other—and Jesus—will grow that much deeper. If you lead these sessions, take a little time to read and get comfortable with them so you can lead in a natural, spontaneous way. Even if you don't have a small group and can't do the group activities, there are still great questions that'll help you process what you learn each week.

By the way, would you like to connect with others from around the world who are doing *Pure Praise*, too? Go to our Facebook page called "Pure Praise Worship Study." You'll find videos and other helpful resources to make your experience of this study even better!

One more thing: As you go through this book each day, you'll notice an icon that looks like this: Whenever you come across this icon, slow down. You'll look up a passage in your Bible, answer a question, pray, or do something else that will require giving God your undivided attention. There's plenty of space to journal, so grab a pen or pencil each time you open this book. Always take time to do these important exercises.

Let's try one now. Stop reading and pray. Yes, *right now*. Take a few moments to ask God to help you learn and grow as you do this study. Thank God for what he's going to reveal to you, and for the way your spiritual life is about to rocket to new heights.

I promise that you're in for the ride of your life—an experience with Jesus that's more exciting and intense than any snowboard halfpipe could ever hope to be! So go for it! Decide now to *go extreme in worshipping God!*

Your friend,
Dwayne Moore

*Please complete both forms below. Keep the top half to remind you of
your commitment.*

I'M GOING EXTREME

Count me in to do this study, *Pure Praise*! With God's help over
the next six weeks, I'll make time five days out of every week
to complete the daily devotional. I'll use my Bible each day and
take time to journal what God's teaching me. I want to be fully
devoted to worshipping the Lord the way he wants me to.

Name: _____

Date: _____

I have asked _____
to hold me accountable to do this study.

*Complete this bottom form, and then tear it off and give it to your youth leader,
pastor, parent, or friend who'll help hold you accountable to finish this study.*

I'M GOING EXTREME

Count me in to do this study, *Pure Praise*! With God's help over
the next six weeks, I'll make time five days out of every week
to complete the daily devotional. I'll use my Bible each day and
take time to journal what God's teaching me. I want to be fully
devoted to worshipping the Lord the way he wants me to.

Name: _____

Date: _____

I have asked _____
to hold me accountable to do this study.

PURE PRAISE
FOR YOUTH

Worship Is a Way of Life

DAY 1

I vividly remember the moment I first realized the awesome power of praise. It was both amazing and life-changing.

During my elementary through high-school years, God used many teachers and mentors to help shape my understanding and encourage my Christian walk. However, it wasn't until college that I met someone who challenged my view of praise. His name was Marty. Marty was known across campus as a guy who passionately loved Jesus—his walk matched his talk.

One day during my freshman year, Marty invited me to gather with a few friends for some praise time. As he played and sang one song after another, something started to happen. Everyone's focus turned away from Marty and toward Jesus. Some songs were familiar to me, others weren't, but they all included thoughts my heart wanted and needed to say to God. I felt as if we were actually standing in God's throne room telling him how awesome he is.

You may have experienced this sort of thing before, maybe not. For me, I had never seen someone go from one song to the next in nonstop, vertical praise for 30 to 40 minutes straight. That day was a holy moment for me, and it gave me a thirst to know God more and worship him with "all that is within me" (Psalm 103:1, KING JAMES VERSION).

Has praising God ever made you want to know him more? If so, write about that experience. If not, write a prayer to God asking him to help you experience that kind of time with him.

JOURNAL

Our Central Passage

The main passage we'll focus on throughout this study is 2 Chronicles 20. It tells a story about the people of Jerusalem and Judah who all had their light-bulb moment at the same time! Three large armies were marching against Jehoshaphat and the people of Judah. Jehoshaphat's response was to call everyone to a giant prayer meeting.

I know, I know—it doesn't sound all that exciting, does it? Why would you stop and have a prayer meeting when you're about to go to war? But wait and see. God does amazing things, and during each week of this study, we'll look at a different part of this incredible story.

 Before going any further, talk to God for a minute. Ask him to open your eyes to see what he wants to show you during the next six weeks.

 Now read 2 Chronicles 20:1-30. This is a long passage; most days won't have this much reading. But hang with me, because we need to read the whole story before we can break it down.

What do you think? Here's a story about a group of people about to get pummeled by their rivals. So what do they do? They pray, and the Lord answers, "Listen, King Jehoshaphat and all who live in Judah and Jerusalem…do not be afraid or discouraged because of this vast army. For the battle is not yours, but God's." (2 Chronicles 20:15). So what do the people of Judah do? They send out the choir in front of the army. Sounds crazy, right? In fact, it sounds as if they're about to bring a whole new meaning to the phrase "sacrifice of praise" (Hebrews 13:15, New Living Translation).

But what we discover in this passage is an incredible worship service. In the midst of very scary circumstances, the people of Judah had a supernatural encounter with almighty God. Why? Because they *chose* to worship. They saw God as he was and therefore worshipped him as they should.

According to Strong's Concordance, the word *worship* means "to bow down, prostrate oneself, before a superior in homage, before God in worship." God is our superior; he is our Lord. The essence of worship is choosing to do life God's way instead of our way. Just as the people of Judah bowed in surrender, we must surrender to Jesus as Lord. Anything less isn't true biblical worship.

 What does it mean for *you* to worship God? How would you define it? Write your definition below.

JOURNAL

Jesus also believed worship was a priority. When he was asked, "Of all the commandments, which is the most important?" Jesus replied, "The most important commandment is this: 'Hear, O Israel! The Lord our God is the one and only Lord. And you must love the Lord your God with all your heart, all your soul, all your mind, and all your strength" (Mark 12:28-30, NLT).

People have asked me, "Isn't the Christian life really just a bunch of *don'ts*? Don't do this. Don't do that." I say to them, "No, the Christian life is really one big YES. Yes God, I will follow you." It's that simple. *Worship* God completely.

Worship isn't just something we do on Sundays at church. And it's definitely more than singing or going to a service, although those are pieces of it. What worship really is…is a *lifestyle*. It involves everything we do—the choices we make, the people we hang out with, and the way we spend our time. It means trying to please God in every part of our lives. As Pastor Rick Warren says, worship is simply "bringing pleasure to God."[1]

In 1 Corinthians 10:31 Paul wrote, "So whether you eat or drink or whatever you do, do it all for the glory of God." Paul's examples show us that our most common daily activities can, and should, bring glory and honor to Jesus.

What are some ways you can worship God every day at home, at school, or at practice? Write your ideas here.

JOURNAL

How can even the most boring things you do bring honor and worship to God? Go ahead and write those, too.

JOURNAL

[1] Rick Warren, *The Purpose Driven Life* (Grand Rapids, MI: Zondervan, 2002), 64.

Keep It Real

During this journey we'll be practicing our praise before God in different and maybe even new and unusual ways. Whenever you practice, it's always good to warm up. As the people of Judah heard Jehoshaphat describe God's faithfulness to them in the past and God's promises for their future, no doubt their hearts started to warm up to praise. So let's stretch our souls right now.

How has God recently shown his grace, mercy, or power in your life? Write about it below.

JOURNAL

Now thank God for how faithful he's already been to you. Then write some things about God that you're thankful for right now in the space below.

JOURNAL

Keep It Pure

Ask God to reveal any actions or attitudes you have that aren't honoring him. Write them down; then ask God to forgive you and help you worship him in everything you do today.

JOURNAL

This week's meditation verses are Deuteronomy 6:4-5. Please write those verses below. As you write, think about what this passage teaches us about worship as a way of life.

JOURNAL

Yesterday we discovered that worship is a lifestyle. Everything in our lives—doing schoolwork, going to practice, driving a car, even eating a cheeseburger—can be an act of worship. But have you stopped to think about *why* God is interested in our everyday stuff?

My wife, Sonia, and I have been blessed with two energetic boys who are three years apart in age. They're not perfect; in fact, if you heard how they fuss and fight, you'd probably say that's an understatement! But even though they're far from being little angels, I'm still convinced that being a dad is the best calling on earth!

Growing up, our boys could make me smile no matter what they were doing. I enjoyed watching them play with their G.I. Joes and Rescue Heroes (remember those?). I used to love hearing them laugh as they watched their favorite cartoons or played in the dirt. Sometimes I'd stand in their rooms late at night and just watch them sleep.

What I want you to see is that those guys never had to be *doing* something to please me. They've always brought me joy and pleasure simply because of *who they are*. They're my *sons*. Come to think about it, the only time they don't please me is when they don't *obey* me.

Have you ever stopped to think that you might actually bring your parents joy just by being their child? That might be hard to believe when they're telling you to clean your room or do the dishes, but you can bring great delight to your parents just because you belong to them.

It's the same way with God. No matter what your relationship is like with your parents on earth, God is always delighted with his children. Do you remember what God said when he finished creating man and woman? He said "it was very good" (Genesis 1:31). Think about that. They hadn't done *anything* yet, but he was still pleased with them. God enjoyed *being* with them. They were made in God's image, which means they reflected what God looks like. They brought him glory simply because of who they were, not because of what they did.

Have you ever felt like you couldn't do enough to please someone? God isn't like that. As God's children, God delights in us for who we are—and *whose* we are. Like Adam and Eve, we are created to praise God with our lives.

Read Ephesians 1:3-14. What phrase does Paul keep repeating here? Don't miss this. Read it again if you need to, to catch it.

Paul repeats this phrase because he wants us to see why we were created. All God has done for us and in us is "to the praise of his glory" (verse 6, KVJ). Amazing as it may sound, God loves us so much that he's raised us up and seated us with Jesus in heavenly realms to show us off as trophies of his grace. Have you ever received a trophy you wanted to show off? You were probably very proud of it. That's how God feels about *you*!

Not only will we be God's trophies in the coming age—we're already living proof of his goodness and mercy. First Peter 2:9 states, "You are a chosen people. You are royal priests, a holy nation, God's very own possession. As a result, you can show others the goodness of God, for he called you out of the darkness into his wonderful light" (NLT). No wonder Jehoshaphat, in his prayer in 2 Chronicles 20, reminded God of how he treated his people in the past. God has always been willing to come through for us.

2 Chronicles 20:29 clearly says the nations feared the *Lord*, rather than the people of Judah. It was the *Lord* who won the battle. God was the one who encouraged the enemy armies to turn on each other. The people of Judah did nothing but obediently "stand still and see the salvation of the Lord" (verse 17, NEW KING JAMES VERSION). The focus was on God and what *he* could do. God got the victory, and God got the glory.

That's the way it should be in every part of our lives. The fact that we're even breathing should remind us of God's grace and goodness. No wonder the people of Judah shouted, "Praise the Lord, for his mercy endures forever" (2 Chronicles 20:21, NKJV). May our lives shout it so loud this world can't help but take notice!

Keep It Real

Spend a few minutes thinking about the passage you read in Ephesians 1:3-14. Let these words fill your heart and mind: *Your life has indescribable purpose—both today and all the way through eternity—beyond what you can think or imagine.*

Why not celebrate right now? This might seem awkward, but I'll bet you already sing your heart out along with the radio when nobody's around! So why not sing for the Lord? He's already watching anyway. You may even want to write out below what's bursting from your heart right now.

JOURNAL

PURE PRAISE
FOR YOUTH

Now check out Romans 12:1-2. God wants our bodies yielded to him, pure and simple. *That's* what's acceptable to God: giving up control and allowing God to do whatever he wants to do in us and through us. As we lay our lives down for God to fill and to use, we become expressions of praise to him. Write a prayer of surrender now.

Worship in All Directions

When you hear the word *worship*, what comes to your mind? Write it down before reading on.

This week we've already seen that true biblical worship includes our entire lives. John MacArthur, Jr. explains in his book *The Ultimate Priority* that for our worship to be "whole-life" it must include three directions: (1) *upward* worship, when we worship God by focusing directly on him (how we normally think of worship), (2) worshipping God *inwardly*, and (3) worshipping God *outwardly*, to those around us.[1] Let's dig deeper into this.

Three Directions of Worship

You might think of three-directional worship like this: Imagine saying to your parents, "You are the best parents to ever walk the face of the earth. I am so thankful for all the chores you give me to do. In fact, I practically worship at your feet just for letting me clean my room and take out the trash." Am I laying it on thick enough yet? I *did* say "imagine," after all.

Now, having said such a mouthful *upward* toward your parents, how should you behave when they're not looking? If you really meant what you said, you'd speak well of your parents and what they make you do even when they aren't around. You'd also work hard and enthusiastically when they aren't watching you. Why? Because *inwardly* you really *do* love your parents and want to please them.

Let's take this one step further. When you've been out with your parents, have they ever told you to be on your best behavior because you represent your family? Again, this shouldn't only happen when you're *with* your parents. Every time you listen to your teacher, treat your friends' parents with respect, or come home in time for curfew, you're *outwardly* honoring your parents. Your actions show how much you respect and appreciate the family you come from.

In much the same way, God is honored—*worshipped*—not only by what we say to him, but also by how much we love him on the inside and by how we respond to every person he died for—which *is* every person. So today, let's take a closer look at the inward and outward directions of worship. Then tomorrow we'll check out my personal favorite, the upward direction.

Again, the *inward* direction of our worship refers to who we are when no one's looking. It's not all that difficult to lift up praises to God when we're at

church or around other Christians. In those places, we're encouraged, maybe even expected, to do so. But what about when we're at home, talking online, or surfing the Internet? Are we careful to please God with our private thoughts, with the things we choose to look at and the places we visit—in person *or* virtually?

Worshipping inwardly with our actions is a good test for our worship. If our hearts' desire is to please God, we'll make an effort to reflect that with our lives. Psalm 51:16-17 says that God wants "a broken and contrite heart" (NKJV) more than outward sacrifice. God knows that if our hearts are purely devoted to him, it can't help but affect our outward behavior.

Read Proverbs 4:23. Why do you think the writer said we're to guard our hearts "above all else"?

A wellspring is the source from which water flows. In the same way, our hearts are the source of our thoughts, motives, and actions. So this inward direction of worship is very, very important.

Reading 2 Chronicles 16:9, we see that God is searching the earth *not* to support those who sing the best or raise their hands the most, but to find those "whose hearts are fully committed to him." Without that commitment to God, all other forms of worship actually make God sick.

If you think that last statement is crazy—or if you're just curious—check out Amos 5:21-23, Psalm 51, and Revelation 3:16. If you're feeling led to write out your thoughts on this, go ahead and skip to "Keep It Real," and write what's on your heart. It's OK to do this now.

So what would it mean for *you* to worship inwardly? Think of some ways you can honor God with your thoughts and motives and in your times alone, and write them down.

JOURNAL

Now, let's think about the *outward* direction of worship. Below are four ways we can bring glory to our Lord outwardly, and they all have to do with our relationships with other people.

First, God is worshipped when we share our faith and when we get a chance to introduce someone to Jesus. In Romans 15:16, Paul says God gave him the "priestly duty of proclaiming the gospel...so that the Gentiles might become an offering acceptable to God." What a privilege to take part in that kind of offering! Once we've helped someone change for all eternity, we'll be hooked on sharing our faith.

Second, we worship God when we help others. How many of us can say that we help out our neighbors, or even our parents and siblings? Most of the time we're just not motivated, or we get so busy that we don't even *notice* who might need help. But as followers of Jesus, we're called to be good Samaritans (Luke 10:30-37). Jesus clearly taught us to give "a cup of cold water" in his name (Matthew 10:42).

 Read Philippians 4:14-19. Look again at verse 18. How does Paul describe the Philippians' gifts? When was the last time you were able to give a gift that was appreciated like that? What was the result?

A third wonderful way to express our love for God is to give money to those in need. When we give, we should be cheerful instead of grudging (2 Corinthians 9:7), because what matters most is the motivation of our hearts. You may not have a lot of money to give right now, but you can give what you have. Do your parents give you spending money, lunch money, or any extra money for the things you do? If you stop and think about it, you probably have access to more funds than you think. Once again, God considers the source of true worship to be our willing and compassionate hearts. It means generously giving what we can.

A fourth way we worship God outwardly is by being sensitive to our weaker brothers and sisters. All of Romans 14 focuses on strong and weak Christians. According to verse 13, we are to "live in such a way that you will not cause another believer to stumble and fall" (NLT). Verse 18 goes on to tell us, "If you serve Christ with this attitude, you will please God" (NLT).

For some reason, my father (who wasn't a Christian) didn't think Christian women should wear shorts. So when I was growing up, I never saw our next-door neighbor wearing shorts. She chose not to wear them in front of my dad because she didn't want to offend him. God is honored through us when we show that kind of selfless sensitivity.

What about you? Have you ever worn something to church that you thought looked perfectly fine, but your parents (or grandparents) thought was inappropriate? You might have thought they were just totally out of touch, but what would have been the selfless thing to do? You guessed it: Just change your clothes. It's not a hard thing to do, but being sensitive to others honors God.

 How might each of the four ways of outward worship play out in your own life?

JOURNAL }

PURE PRAISE
FOR YOUTH

Because our entire study is based on 2 Chronicles 20, I want to close this session by focusing on Jehoshaphat. "Jehoshaphat was a good king, following the example of his father, Asa. He did what was pleasing in the Lord's sight" (1 Kings 22:43, NLT). He was obviously a man of character, a good man on the *inside*. He also respected his people and taught them the word of God (2 Chronicles 17:7). He protected them. In fact, he had more than a million men ready and willing to fight in his army! No wonder he was "highly esteemed" by the people (2 Chronicles 17:5, NLT). To sum it up, Jehoshaphat not only said he loved and honored God, but also showed it by his actions. He worshipped God with his *whole* life. How about you?

Keep It Real

Hebrews 4:12 says "the word of God…exposes our innermost thoughts and desires" (NLT). Who are you *really*? Where don't your inside and outside match? Write your honest thoughts to God below.

JOURNAL

Keep It Pure

Make a choice today to intentionally worship God outwardly. Review the four ways of praising outwardly, and commit to acting on just one of them today. Ask God to help you worship with your whole life today.

Write out this week's meditation verses, Deuteronomy 6:4-5. Then write them again in your own words.

JOURNAL

WEEK 1 | DAY 3

---

[1] *The Ultimate Priority*, John McArthur, (Chicago, IL: Moody Press, 1983), 14-16.

Going *Up*—Thanksgiving and Praise

As we saw yesterday, worship is three-directional: inward, outward, and upward. Hebrews 13:15-16 touches on all three of these. ✒ Please read that passage now. Write down the word or words that could represent each of those three directions. And note how the passage ends—"for with such sacrifices God is pleased."

JOURNAL

Today we're going to look at worship pointed *upward*, toward God. It's what most people think of when they hear the word *worship*. In Hebrews 13:15 the upward direction involves two specific actions: praise and thanksgiving: "Let us continually offer the sacrifice of praise to God, that is, the fruit of our lips, giving thanks to His name" (NKJV). Praise is primarily recognizing God for who he *is*. Thanksgiving, on the other hand, is giving thanks to God for what he's *done*. Next week we'll focus on understanding praise better. Today we'll look at why thankfulness is so important.

We can be sure nothing ever happens to us that our loving God doesn't allow. After all, just as God protected Moses, God protects us "in the cleft of the rock" as he covers us with his mighty hand (Exodus 33:22, NKJV). Knowing that God corrects us and provides protection and direction should give us comfort all the time. But let's be honest: We know we should be humbly grateful, yet there are times when we're tempted to be "grumbly hateful"!

I once heard a pastor share a story of a young couple who went to the hospital to have their baby. Complications came up. Tests results showed their child had Down syndrome. Word spread throughout the hospital about this young couple and their yet-to-be-born baby.

Word had also gotten around that these parents were Christians. So several nurses and other hospital staff began to speculate about how these "God-fearing" people would respond. The hospital switchboard operator even listened in on the couple's private phone conversations. What she heard would change her life forever. Rather than being bitter and doubting God, the young mother just kept stating her trust and thankfulness in her Lord. She said that no matter what, they knew God would work the situation out for their good and his glory.

Not only did that operator give her life to Jesus, but as a result of those parents' faith, more than twenty nurses and doctors walked down the aisle of that couple's church the following Sunday and trusted in Jesus!

That new mom and dad understood that God would be with them in the midst of unexpected or difficult circumstances. Before any of us can give thanks and praise to God and really mean it, we too must accept in our hearts that God is in control.

There is a throne in heaven. And it is *occupied*! Our great God, our mighty and majestic Father, is sitting on that throne right now. This world may seem as if it's spinning out of control, but God is still the all-powerful, all-knowing, ever-present King of kings and Lord of lords. And guess what? That same God loves you and me.

Stop right now and thank God for loving and watching over you at this very moment.

Turn to 1 Thessalonians 5:18. Write it out word for word.

JOURNAL

This passage means that we don't just give thanks *for* our circumstances, but also *in* them. We're probably not going to *feel* thankful for problems and hardships that come our way. However, if we clearly understand that God reigns and is using our circumstances to make us more like him and bring him greater glory, we can be thankful *to* him constantly, even while we're going through the tough times.

Have you ever read the book *Hermie: A Common Caterpillar* by Max Lucado? It's the story of two caterpillars named Hermie and Wormie. They're common caterpillars—so common and uninteresting, in fact, that they don't even have any stripes or spots. When they complain to God about their commonness, God reminds them that he's not finished with them yet. He's giving them new hearts, he tells them. This makes them feel better for a while, but each time they meet an insect with a unique ability they wish they had, they begin complaining again. (Sound familiar?) Eventually Hermie decides to simply be thankful for how God made him, and that same night he turns into a beautiful butterfly! His heart, though, had already been changed.

Let's focus on having an attitude of gratitude. What's going on in your life now that you need to be thankful for? Take some time to write down every blessing you think of. And remember, blessings can also be disguised as disappointments.

JOURNAL

Talk to God about anything in your life that you're finding hard to give thanks for right now. Be honest and open with God; he already knows what you're feeling anyway. Ask God to help you find a way to be thankful in that situation. Ask God to change your heart. Then decide to be *thankful* throughout your day today, deliberately looking for God's presence in each and every circumstance. Write your prayer in the space below.

JOURNAL

Try to write Deuteronomy 6:4-5 from memory (or least write as much as you can remember!). Afterward, look it up in your Bible to see whether what you wrote is accurate.

JOURNAL

My wife has a green thumb. She loves and cares for her plants. She makes sure they get everything they need to be healthy and happy (if plants can be happy). Sometimes she moves a plant closer to a window if she sees it isn't getting enough sunlight. It always amazes me how quickly the plants perk up and look healthy (and happy) again.

Worshipping God is kind of like that. We can't encounter God's presence and awesome glory and not *somehow* be changed.

Let's look again at the story of Jehoshaphat and the people of Judah. Read 2 Chronicles 20:2-4. How would you have felt if you'd gotten this news?

Now read verses 17-19. Check out the attitude of the people of Judah *after* God spoke through his prophet.

What made the people of Judah go from shaking with fear to shouting with joy? One big wonderful word: *God*. God showed up in that place, and their entire outlook changed. The people of Judah were full of fear as they gathered to seek God, but they left full of faith.

In Psalm 73 a guy named Asaph goes through a similar change because of worship. Read Psalm 73:2-14. Why is Asaph so negative in these verses? How would you have reacted to these circumstances?

Now, read verses 18-28. See how Asaph's whole focus changed? He went from being so discouraged that he wanted to quit, to realizing what's going to happen to the wicked in the end. He said, "Earth has nothing I desire besides you" (verse 25). In fact, Asaph suddenly turned all his attention toward God. He barely mentioned God's name in the first half of this chapter, but then Asaph prayed directly to God. Talk about a major attitude adjustment!

Please read the three verses we skipped (15-17). What did Asaph do that totally changed his outlook? Write about that here.

JOURNAL

Another great example of how worship changes us is in Isaiah 6. At the beginning of this chapter, Isaiah was sad over the death of his friend King Uzziah. Through a vision, Isaiah found himself right in the middle of a heavenly worship service. He "saw the Lord, high and exalted, seated on a throne" (verse 1). He went on to describe the seraphim all calling to one another, "Holy, holy, holy is the Lord Almighty." Their voices were so loud that the entire place shook. The temple was filled with smoke, representing the presence of God.

Can you imagine what that service must have been like? Wouldn't you love to have been there with Isaiah? The thing is, Isaiah wasn't actually in the service—at first. Verse 1 says he "saw the Lord." He was an observer, just checking things out. Maybe he was like some people you see at church who don't really participate. They just watch and check things out. But even wallflowers are affected when God shows up! That's what happened to Isaiah. He couldn't sit on the sidelines for long.

Read Isaiah 6:5-8. Do you relate to Isaiah's immediate reaction? Why or why not? What about his response in verse 8?

When God's light of perfect holiness shines on us, it always shows us how unholy we are. In God's presence, Isaiah's sin was more than he could stand. You see, God never points out our sin to condemn us. He shows us our sin so we, like Isaiah, can admit it and turn away from it. He "touches our lips" and hearts, and he forgives us.

Isaiah went from being a downcast and reluctant worship spectator to a willing participant in anything God wanted him to do. He didn't even wait to be singled out—he enthusiastically volunteered. That's the amazing change God can make in your life through worship!

Keep It Real

In Psalm 63:2 David wrote, "I have seen you in the sanctuary and beheld your power and your glory." Do you remember a quiet time or a worship service when God gave you a glimpse of his glory? If so, how did it affect you? How did it change you? Write about it below. If you can't think of a time like this, write a prayer to God asking him to reveal his glory to you and speak to you.

JOURNAL

PURE PRAISE
FOR YOUTH

Now think about a song that expresses your praise and thanksgiving to the Lord. Sing it or speak it to God now.

Keep It Pure

What has God revealed to you that you need to confess or commit to him? Write a prayer to God asking him to change you. Be sure to thank God for meeting with you today and showing you a glimpse of his awesome glory and grace.

JOURNAL

Write Deuteronomy 6:4-5 from memory below. Check in your Bible to be sure you got everything right.

JOURNAL

For this session, you'll need:

- Empty paper towel rolls
- Chenille wires
- Colored markers
- Stickers
- Construction paper
- Toothpicks
- Old magazines
- Photos of your group members (if possible)
- Scissors
- Tape or glue

GET CONNECTED (15 minutes)

Thanks for being here today! I'm excited about this series we're launching into today. Because we're going to spend a lot of time interacting with each other over the next six weeks, let's start right now. Stand up and get into groups of three.

Allow time for groups to form. If you're meeting for the first time, give group members a few minutes to introduce themselves to each other before moving on. Distribute supplies and tools to groups.

For the next few minutes, I'd like each of you to build a "trophy" that reflects who you are and the things you do well. Maybe your trophy reflects your sports skills, your academic abilities, your artistic streak, your mechanical talents, or your skill at making other people feel valued and appreciated. As you're working on your trophies, discuss these questions with the rest of your group: → →1

Give groups 10 minutes to build their trophies and discuss the questions, and then regain everyone's attention, keeping them with their groups. Ask for volunteers from each group to share.

The more we understand the importance of worshipping God through everything we do in life, the more we become "trophies of God's grace." Each talent, skill, or ability represented by these trophies is a way we can worship God. Let's dig deeper to see what it means to pursue and develop a lifestyle of worship.

DIG DEEPER (20 minutes)

Discuss together: → →2

Turn back to your groups. Have a volunteer read Hebrews 13:15-16, and then take 10 minutes to discuss these questions: → →3

PURE PRAISE
FOR YOUTH

→ → **1**
- Why did you choose this specific skill or ability as your inspiration?
- In this week's readings, Dwayne talked about how God sees us as "trophies of his grace." How have you experienced God's grace in your life?

- How easy or difficult is it to see yourself as a trophy of God's grace? Why?

→ → **2**
- Think of someone who has a highly specialized career: a professional athlete, a world-class musician, or a best-selling author. How would that person's career affect every other area of his or her life?

HEBREWS 13:15-16

→ → **3**
- When do you find it easiest to choose God's way instead of yours? When is it hardest?

- How would your life be different if you fully put these verses into practice? Throw some ideas out there.

Bring everyone back together after 10 minutes. Share highlights and insights from your discussion time.

This week's meditation verses are Deuteronomy 6:4-5. Who'd like to read them for us? → → 4

BRING IT TO LIFE (20 minutes)

God wants our lives to be defined by how—and how much—we worship him. Everything we do can be an act of worship if we choose to have a God-honoring attitude and perspective.

Read 1 Corinthians 10:31, and then discuss these questions. → → 5

Get back into your groups, and take five minutes to discuss these questions. I'll close us in prayer afterward. → → 6

After five minutes, regain everyone's attention. Pray for the group, asking God to remind each person about the importance and rewards of leading lifestyles of worship in the coming week—and truly making it a lifestyle.

DEUTERONOMY 6:4-5

→ → 4 • Why isn't God satisfied with our loving him with *some* or *most* of our heart, soul, and strength? When have you seen or experienced this less-than-whole-self approach to God?

1 CORINTHIANS 10:31

→ → 5 • How can our most common daily activities bring glory and honor to Jesus? Give some examples.

• How easy or difficult would it be for you to approach those activities as ways to worship God? Why?

→ → 6 • How have your ideas about leading a lifestyle of worship—and about what worship *is*—been changed or challenged this week?

• How will you respond to those challenges this week?

PRAISING GOD

DAY 1

The Priority of Praise

Have you ever flown in an airplane? Do you remember what you thought the first time you looked out the window and saw the clouds and earth below? If it was a clear day, you probably saw, as birds might, for miles on end! I think it'd be good for *us* to take a birds-eye view of praise to God before going any further.

Let's start here: When you think of praising God, what comes to mind? A lot of people seem to think that praise is something you do when you're at church or at a concert with a rocking worship band. To other Christians, the idea of praising the Lord seems foreign and a bit odd.

So let's imagine that we're flying over and looking down at this thing called praise. As we do, I think you'll realize that praise isn't strange or uncommon at all, and it's not restricted to Christian events. Like the land and water seen from an airplane, praise to our great God stretches as far as the mind can grasp and beyond, in all directions. It is infinitely vast; praise is everywhere we look.

As we continue our overview of the "landscape of praise," we'll see many landmarks that help give a clear picture of just how far praise to God goes. Let's look at five of those landmarks now.

1. God's people have always praised him. In Psalm 33, the opening words to the call to worship include, "Sing joyfully to the Lord, you righteous; it is fitting for the upright to praise him" (verse 1). Israel's most shining moments occurred when the people of Israel lifted up God in praise. David said that God is the praise of Israel (Psalm 22:3). And we've already seen that "all the people of Judah and Jerusalem fell down in worship before the Lord," and that some Levites praised God with loud voices (2 Chronicles 20:18-19).

Whether they were kneeling quietly or being loud and joyful, the people of Judah never considered what they were doing as weird or inappropriate (even before a God they couldn't see!). Rather, it was their most natural response to God's power and grace.

2. Throughout the Bible we can find praise being offered to God. The word *praise* can be found more than 200 times in the Bible. When we include related

PURE PRAISE
FOR YOUTH

words and phrases such as *worship, sing, shout,* and *bow down,* that number climbs to almost 500! Clearly, praising God isn't an unusual idea.

3. For all eternity, God will be praised. Jude 1:25 says, "All glory to him who alone is God, our Savior through Jesus Christ our Lord. All glory, majesty, power, and authority are his before all time, and in the present, and beyond all time! Amen" (NEW LIVING TRANSLATION). *How* long? Always and forever! Praise in heaven is *ongoing,* both in the present and in the *never-ending* future!

4. Throughout all creation, God will be praised. Read Revelation 5:11-14. What do you think it would be like to be in the middle of this experience?

According to Philippians 2:9-11, even the demons will have to bow and confess that Jesus is Lord! Obviously, praise is both pleasing to God and something that should come naturally to his creation.

5. At this very moment in heaven, God is being praised! Praise to our holy God is so important that heaven itself never stops doing it! According to Revelation 4:8, the four living creatures "never stop saying, 'Holy, holy, holy is the Lord God Almighty.'" Even if no one around you seems interested in praising, be encouraged! There's a loud roar of praise to God in heaven at the *exact* moment you're praising him. So go ahead—sing and play really loud!

Read back over these five landmarks. Which ones stand out to you as great reasons to praise God? On the other hand, which landmarks seem to go over your head? Stop and ask God for understanding right now. Write out your prayer and what God's showing you right now.

Not only is praise infinitely vast, it is *inevitable*. While God desires praise from his people, he *demands* it from his creation. One way or another, God will be praised. David said, "The heavens declare the glory of God" (Psalm 19:1, KING JAMES VERSION). That means every day of every year of every century, God's creation is proclaiming his greatness and worth.

Do you remember Jesus' words to the Pharisees when they told him to quiet his noisy disciples at his triumphal entry? " 'I tell you,' [Jesus] replied, 'if they keep quiet, the stones will cry out' " (Luke 19:40, NLT). I'm sure I speak for both of us when I say I don't want any rocks taking my place! God is going to get the praise he deserves...period.

Keep It Real

Read all of Revelation 5. Every time you come to a song that's sung around the throne of God, read it out loud with conviction, as though you're right there with them! If you know Jesus, you'll be in that scene one day, so you might as well get some practice!

Keep It Pure

The meditation verse for this week is Psalm 119:164. Please write it below. Think about how you can apply it to your life this week.

JOURNAL

Last week we saw that we should worship God through everything we do. Every time we breathe in and out, it can be an expression of worship—*breathing* is already a statement about how loving and faithful God is to us. We also learned that praise is only one part of worship. Praise is *upward* focus toward God. Put another way: While all acceptable praise is worship, not all worship is praise.

When our hearts are on fire with love for God, a lot of times we'll worship him by whatever we're doing at that moment without even realizing it! When we breathe, we don't usually think about it. But we're almost sure to be aware of any time we praise. That's because praise is *deliberate*. Every time we praise the Lord, it's because we've made a *choice*.

What are ways you can (or already do) deliberately give praise to God when you're at school, at home, or talking or texting with your friends?

JOURNAL

Let's look at a group of children in the Bible who made a conscious choice to praise Jesus. Read Matthew 21:14-16. Why do you think these kids were so excited and uninhibited in their praise?

JOURNAL

Remember in 2 Chronicles 20 how the people of Judah praised and celebrated the Lord? In the same way, these children praised and celebrated Jesus being there with them. No doubt to some watching that day, what these children were doing looked a bit foolish, even annoying or inappropriate. Yet when the religious leaders got angry, Jesus defended the children. He said, "Out of the mouth of babes and nursing infants, You have perfected praise" (NEW KING JAMES VERSION). Those kids were offering the kind of praise all of us should give to God.

Perfect Praise

What makes our praise to God "perfect"? First, perfect praise starts on the inside and then flows "out of the mouth." It comes from a heart that worships God passionately. Second, for our praise to be perfect, we must come to God as if we were small children. God wants to see certain childlike qualities in us. For instance, little children are humble. Jesus said, "Whoever humbles himself as this little child is the greatest in the kingdom of heaven" (Matthew 18:4, NKJV). Children are also very trusting. We must trust God when we're praising, no matter what the circumstances.

There's one more thing about these children that made their praise perfect and acceptable to God. It's summed up in one very important word that Jesus said: "Out of the mouth of babes and infants, *You*..." The "You" Jesus referred to was God himself. For our praise to be perfect to God, we must depend on God to start our praise and make it perfect. It was God who put it in the hearts of those little ones to dance around, shouting and celebrating King Jesus in the Temple. The Father was perfectly blessed by their praises because *he* set up the entire moment! It was a slam-dunk. God started their praise, and then he led it! There was *no* doubt their praise was accepted by the one who matters most—our audience of one—God!

I was in Salt Lake City a few years ago, leading music for a group of students on their mission trip. Every morning after worship service, we'd go out into the community to share our faith. One day while riding to our assigned area, everyone in the bus started singing praise songs. We sang and sang. The girl beside me was one of those Christians who has "the glow that shows." Her smile was absolutely contagious. I couldn't help but notice that she kept smiling even while she was singing.

At the end of one of our songs, she looked up at me and said the most incredible thing. She said, "You know, I don't sing very well." She paused for a moment, the whole time maintaining that amazing smile. Then she said, "But that's OK with me, because I figure this: God made my voice. And since he made my voice, he must like to hear it." Then her smile got even bigger and brighter, and she said,

"So I'm just gonna sing as loud as I can!"

That girl made a *choice* to praise God with her voice. It didn't matter to her if others thought she was fanatical or uncool. What motivated her was nothing less than passionate love for and devotion to her Lord. A good way to define praise is "the bubbling over of a hot heart." That teenage girl had a hot heart for God. Praise was literally bubbling out of her! And her praise was *perfect*.

Keep It Real

Make the *choice* to praise God right now. Choose one of God's attributes, such as his love, mercy, power, or justice. Tell God *out loud* that you love him and praise him for that quality. Write down what you just prayed, so you can look back on this time later.

JOURNAL

Keep It Pure

If we want to be sure God gets pleasure from our praise, we must get ourselves out of the way and pray a prayer like David's: "O Lord, open my lips and my mouth shall show forth Your praise" (Psalm 51:15, NKJV). Ask God to show you what you need to do to offer *perfect* praise to him from now on.

JOURNAL

Write Psalm 119:164 below. Try saying it from memory.

JOURNAL

Ways to Praise

Have you ever thought how strange praise must appear to those who don't know Jesus? After all, why would anyone want to sing and carry on to a God they can't see or touch? People around you may never know you're worshipping God as you go about your daily activities. But if anyone happens to be nearby when you're compelled to praise, they'll not only notice you, they'll probably wonder what you could possibly be doing!

Say, for example, you're sitting in a car at a red light. You've got your favorite praise song blaring. Before you know it, you're lost in the moment. You start lifting your hands, singing at the top of your lungs. Imagine what the person in the car next to you must be thinking. He or she can't hear what you're singing, but what that person *sees* is definitely an attention-getter!

Praise, by its very nature, is outward, open, and *obvious*. In Psalm 40:3, David said, "He put a new song in my mouth, a hymn of praise to our God. Many will see and fear and put their trust in the Lord." We're on this earth to make God known through our praise! What a privilege! What a responsibility! So we'd better explore every avenue available to us.

Ways to Praise

There are eight ways we can praise. In his book *The Hallelujah Factor*, Jack R. Taylor grouped these ways into three categories to make them easier to remember. One category is *vocal*, which includes singing, shouting, and sharing our faith. A second category is *audible*, which includes clapping and playing an instrument. A third category doesn't involve sound. That group, called *visible*, includes kneeling, dancing, and raising our hands.[1] Today we'll look at this last group.

Read Matthew 2:11. What did their physical response indicate about their hearts?

JOURNAL

Kneeling is both obvious and deliberate. There's something incredibly humbling and powerfully worshipful about bowing down before our great Master.

Another way we can praise God is through *dancing*. Psalm 149:3 says, "Let them praise his name with dancing." Like anything else we do, dancing can be

PURE PRAISE
FOR YOUTH

done for the wrong motives and in the wrong ways. But genuine, joyful dancing before God, and *for* God, is pleasing to him and a great way to praise.

One other visible form of praise is *raising our hands*. I love what Psalm 63:4 says: "I will praise you as long as I live, and in your name I will lift up my hands." Psalm 134:2 encourages us to "Lift up your hands in the sanctuary and praise the Lord." When Jehoshaphat appointed the singers to go out at the head of the army, he told them to "Give thanks to the Lord" (2 Chronicles 20:21b). In the original Hebrew language, these words included the meaning to "throw up your hands." Let's get the picture here: Imagine thousands of musicians leading the army, singing at the top of their lungs with hands stretched toward the sky!

I remember how I felt the first time I saw my one-year-old son looking up at me with his big blue eyes as he held out his hands toward me. I stopped everything I was doing and reached down to hold him! I believe that's what our heavenly Father wants to do with us when we reach our hands—and hearts—up for him.

Keep It Real

Today we begin our "daily exercises" in the eight ways to praise. Many never feel free to praise God when they're around others because they rarely praise him in private. So today, make sure you're alone and no one is watching. It's just you and God.

Give this a try: Kneel where you are before the Lord. Raise both your hands before him. While your hands are lifted, sing one of your favorite praise songs to God, or simply tell him how much you love him.

Keep It Pure

1 Timothy 2:8 says we should lift up *holy* hands to God in prayer. So let's get holy. Confess any sins you haven't already brought to God. Thank God for his forgiveness, and ask him to help you keep your hands and your heart clean today.

Write a prayer of surrender and praise to God.

JOURNAL

[1] Jack R. Taylor, *The Hallelujah Factor* (Nashville, TN: Broadman Press, 1983), 12-13.

Vocal Praise

Yesterday we learned about three visible ways to praise. (Quick—can you name them?) There are also three *vocal* ways to praise. Let's start today with *shouting*.

Growing up, my family went to a rather quiet, reserved church. Only a few people ever raised their hands or said "amen" aloud during service. Some might say we were a "sleepy" church. But there was one lady, Aunt Bessie, who managed to wake us up from time to time. Every fifth Sunday or so, she'd let out a loud shout of praise! Aunt Bessie loved God passionately and walked closely with him. Whenever she got happy, the rest of us knew God was up to something, so we'd better sit up and take notice!

Ezra 3 describes an awesome scene in which a multitude of people started shouting. The children of Israel had only recently returned from exile. Their first temple had been destroyed years before, and now they were rebuilding it. When they saw that the foundation of the new temple had been laid, they sang to the Lord "with praise and thanksgiving." They all gave a great shout of praise to the Lord. In fact, the weeping and shouting were so loud that even people far away could hear it!

Have you ever sat inside a football stadium when the home team scored a touchdown? The celebration shouts are deafening. Wouldn't it be incredible if the next time someone comes to Jesus in our church we all stood up and shouted something like, "*Touchdown*, Jesus!"?

Psalm 5:11 says, "Let them ever shout for joy because You defend them" (NKJV). Shouting isn't just for a few people like Aunt Bessie to do occasionally, but for all of us whom the Lord defends, and we are to do it for-"ever."

A second vocal way to praise is *singing*. Singing is by far the most common of all the ways Christians praise.

Read Psalm 100:2. Why do you think God wants to hear joyful songs?

JOURNAL

Every time we sing God's praise it should be full of joy! Seriously: How can any song about God or our salvation be depressing? We're not off the hook if we're having a bad day or week. We should still sing with gladness. Why? Because

PURE PRAISE
FOR YOUTH

we have hope in God! Psalm 42:5 says, "Why am I discouraged? Why is my heart so sad? I will put my hope in God! I will praise him again—my Savior and my God" (NLT).

One more way we can praise vocally is by *sharing our faith*—telling others what God has done for us. Psalm 107:2 says, "Let the redeemed of the Lord say so" (KJV).

I'll never forget what I witnessed one night while leading praise. I saw like never before the impact someone's Jesus story can have. We were about to finish what had been a rather dry and uneventful worship service. Then, toward the back of the church, one little lady who looked to be in her eighties slowly stood up. Her words were brief and to the point. She simply wanted everyone to know her Lord has always been faithful to her. One by one, others began to stand up, too. (Coming back from the dead was more like it!) Each shared how faithful God has been in their lives. People started flooding to the front of the room. Forty-five minutes later, the service was still going strong! And it all started when a little lady, as Psalm 107 encourages all of us to do, "said so."

Keep It Real

Continuing with our daily praise exercises, sing a song to God *out loud* right now. Then look for someone to share Jesus with today. Talk about Jesus' goodness to you.

Keep It Pure

Ask God to help you see other ways you can vocally express your praise today. Commit your day to God, and tell God you'll trust him for the outcome. Write out your prayer below.

JOURNAL

Say the meditation verse for this week, Psalm 119:164, from memory. Then jot down seven specific times today (or tomorrow) when you could plan to praise God in some way, no matter where you are.

JOURNAL

Audible Praise

We've discussed visible and vocal ways to praise. There are two more ways. These don't involve our voices, but they can still be heard. They are known as audible praise. Let's consider the first one: *playing an instrument.*

🐦 Read Psalm 150. Why do you think so many sounds are included here?

Did you happen to notice that these instruments represent all the major instrument groups in an orchestra? Included in Psalm 150 are brass, wind, string, and percussion instruments. This isn't the first time instruments are mentioned in the Bible. When God delivered Israel from Pharaoh's army, Miriam took a tambourine in her hand and sang and danced to the Lord (Exodus 15:20-21).

More and more churches are using orchestras, drums, guitars, and other nontraditional instruments in their services. Some people say these churches are trying to appeal to the younger generation. While that may be true in part, I prefer to believe they're also trying to return to what some very *old* generations used, particularly those of David's generation. David's band made use of whatever instruments were available.

Have you ever heard someone say, "That guy just worships his guitar"? Fact is, some people will only participate in praise if the worship team uses instruments they happen to like. But David ends Psalm 150 with "let everything that has breath praise the Lord" (NKJV). He realized it is the person playing the instrument (the one with "breath") who praises God.

It's not about the instruments. *They* don't do the praising—*we* do. Instruments are merely tools. It shouldn't matter if it's a piano, a pipe organ, or a ukulele! If we love Jesus, we'll praise him just the same—no matter what we're using to make the music.

Another way to praise is *clapping* to the Lord. Psalm 47:1 says, "Come, everyone! Clap your hands! Shout to God with joyful praise!" (NLT). *Everyone.* Yet, according to Isaiah 55:12, "The trees of the field will clap their hands." And Psalm 98:8 declares, "Let the floods clap their hands" (KJV).

If God is pleased with trees and floods doing it, how much more would he love to hear *us* clapping? Don't worry if you don't always clap perfectly on the beat. The important thing is to clap with joy in your heart, to your awesome Creator!

Some Closing Thoughts

Before we finish this week, I want to make two things clear. First, not everybody is going to agree with how you choose to praise. They may even want to discourage you from trying some of the ways we've learned about. But keep in mind: Our goal is obedience to God. What *God* says is what we'll do, no matter what those around us think or say.

On the other hand, I've heard Bible teachers and preachers say that each of these ways to praise is actually a command we *have* to do if we are to please God. That's not true, either. God's only requirement is that we *praise* him. We have eight wonderful ways to do that, and we should be encouraged to try all of them. Based on our personalities, some will work better for us than others.

But I do want to emphasize this: Just because certain expressions of worship may seem strange or uncomfortable is no reason not to at least *try* them. Remember, the Bible says praise is a "sacrifice" (Hebrews 13:15).

Keep It Real

Think of an upbeat praise song you know. Sing it out loud before God right now. As you sing, try clapping your hands along with it. This may feel awkward if you lack rhythm, but try it anyway. Clap loudly! Finish your song by clapping your praise to the Lord the way you'd clap for a great artist or sports star. Since God is much bigger and more awesome, your clapping should be even noisier!

Keep It Pure

Some of the expressions of praise we've studied this week might feel uncomfortable, unnecessary, or even strange and "beneath you." If so, please go back and reread the Scriptures about those particular expressions. Then pray a prayer of surrender to God concerning your praise life. Ask God to help you willingly and joyfully try all eight ways to praise.

What has God taught you this week that has helped you and challenged you more than anything else?

JOURNAL

Write this week's meditation verse, Psalm 119:164, from memory.

JOURNAL

For this session, you'll need:

- Notecards
- Pens or pencils
- Cup
- Pitcher of water
- Larger container to hold the cup (and the overflowing water)

GET CONNECTED (15 minutes)

Get into groups of four. After groups have formed, distribute notecards (seven per group) and pens or pencils.

The meditation verse this week is Psalm 119:164. Could I have a volunteer read the verse for us? Pause as your volunteer reads.

In this verse, the writer says he praised God seven times each day. Let's see if we can think of seven different ways to praise God. With your group, write a different way to praise God on each of your notecards.

Allow a couple of minutes for groups to talk and write. Then have each group choose one of their cards and act out a charade that demonstrates that action or activity. The other groups will attempt to guess what was described on the card. When you're finished, discuss these questions together: → →1

Give groups ten minutes, and then bring everyone back together. Ask for volunteers to share their answers—and maybe even some of their charades!

Most of us can find at least seven reasons each day to praise God. This psalm reminds us that we need to have an attitude focused on praising God, whether we're having good days *or* bad days. The more intentional we are in trying to find reasons to praise God, the more easily we'll find them. Let's learn more about how we can do that.

DIG DEEPER (25 minutes)

Turn back to your groups. Read Colossians 2:6-7, and then discuss these questions. → →2

PURE PRAISE
FOR YOUTH

→ → **1** • When has your praise of God *felt* like a charade? Why?

• How might praising God throughout your day help make your praise—and each day—more meaningful?

 COLOSSIANS 2:6-7

→ → **2** • Why does being rooted in Jesus help us to be more thankful? When have you experienced this?

• This week, you read about a teenager on a mission trip who sang loudly, joyfully, and intentionally—praise was literally bubbling out of her. What's bubbling or spilling out of your life this week—good *or* bad? Talk about it.

Bring everyone back together after ten minutes. Ask for a volunteer from each group to share from their discussion time.

Bring out your large container, and set it on the floor or on a table. Place the cup inside the container. Take the pitcher of water and begin to slowly pour water into the cup.

Think of this cup as your life. The more you grow in your relationship with God—represented by the water I'm pouring into the cup—the more likely God's praise will overflow in your life. If we stop growing, we stop being filled. God wants us to lead the kind of lives where our praises overflow and are obvious to all the people around us.

Let group members take turns pouring water into the cup and watching it overflow into the container. Then discuss. → → 3

BRING IT TO LIFE (15 minutes)

Get back into your groups one more time. Read Luke 19:36-40, and take ten minutes to discuss these questions. → → 4

Bring everyone back together after 10 minutes. Share highlights and insights from your discussion time.

Pray that each member of your group would continue developing a deeper relationship with God and that the praises for God would overflow and be seen by the people around them.

→ → **3** • Think once more about what's been spilling out of you this week. How might praising God more regularly help more good things spill out of your life?

LUKE 19:36-40

→ → **4** • Why do you think God gives us the opportunity to *choose* to praise him instead of *forcing* us to praise him?

• This week, Dwayne shared about different ways to praise God—vocal, audible, and visible. Which kind of praise is easiest for you, and why? Which comes hardest, and why?

• What steps can you take in the coming week to make your praise for God—in all forms—a consistent part of your daily life?

KNOWING GOD

DAY 1

The One, True God

Do you realize we could spend our entire lives learning about God and still not come close to knowing everything? The reason is simple: God is far beyond our ability to comprehend. Paul summed it up when he wrote, "Have you ever come on anything quite like this extravagant generosity of God, this deep, deep wisdom? It's way over our heads. We'll never figure it out. Is there anyone around who can explain God? Anyone smart enough to tell him what to do?" (Romans 11:33-35, THE MESSAGE).

I want to share an experience that happened while I was a junior in high school. My friend and I were on a mission trip in New Jersey. One night, while eating at a small pizza place, we spotted two guys standing by their cars and talking in the parking lot. We decided to go share Jesus with them.

What happened next caught my friend and me totally off guard. As soon as we introduced ourselves and talked about the church services we were leading, one of the two looked directly at me and said, "I'll come on one condition."

"OK," I replied, "what is it?"

"Do you worship Jehovah God or Almighty God?"

We thought fast and said, "Well, we actually worship both; they're one and the same."

"Then I'm not coming to your church," he said defiantly. "I only worship the Almighty God."

For the next 30 minutes or so, he proceeded to explain all his "reasons" for only worshipping the "Almighty God." He spouted opinion after opinion and even quoted a few verses—out of context, I might add! He was so convincing, in fact, that at one point my friend who was supposed to be helping me said, "Oh yeah, we believe that, too!" I wanted to elbow him and say, "Hush up! We don't believe *any* of this garbage!" Unfortunately, I had little more than opinions about God myself. That guy actually knew more verses than I did!

That conversation woke me up to just how little I knew about God. I sat up until after midnight that evening searching through my Bible for every description of God I could find. I realized I could no longer accept someone else's ideas as

my own. I had to know for myself, but not so I could win the next debate on God or Christianity. Rather, God compelled me to come to know the *true* God, the one God of the Bible.

Do you remember the story in 1 Kings 18 where Elijah confronted the prophets of Baal? He challenged them to a test. Whichever god—theirs or his—answered by fire, *that* was the true God. From morning until night the prophets of Baal begged their god to answer them. They even cut themselves and shouted frantically. But no fire ever fell on their altar. To up the ante, Elijah had twelve large jars of water poured on the offering!

Read 1 Kings 18:36-39. What does this tell you about Elijah? About God?

Unfortunately, unlike Elijah, some of us need to be reminded that God *is* God (and we're not).

When Jehoshaphat and the people of Judah learned that three armies were marching toward them, they prayed to God. God heard them and answered. He saved them from destruction. Only the one, true God could have done that. We should settle for no other God but our true and living God and Savior!

Keep It Real

When Jehoshaphat prayed, he did three things. First, he *praised God* for how great he is. Second, he *remembered* some ways God had been faithful to his people in the past. Finally, he boldly *reminded God* of his promises.

Take time and pray like that to the Lord right now for yourself or someone you know. Praise him *out loud* where you are.

Keep It Pure

There is one word that Jehoshaphat and Elijah had in common, one word that's absolutely necessary for our worship to be pleasing. That word is *faith*. Hebrews 11:6 says, "Without faith it is impossible to please Him, for he who comes to God must believe that He is" (NEW KING JAMES VERSION). Stop now and ask God to show you where you're not completely trusting in him. Write down what God shows you.

JOURNAL

WEEK 3 | DAY 1

This week's meditation verse is Philippians 3:10. Read it over slowly three times. Now, make it personal by writing it as your prayer to God.

JOURNAL

Transcendent God

Yesterday we focused on how there is no other God but the Lord. But do you realize that even the demons believe that? The Bible says they not only believe it, but that they literally tremble before him (James 2:19).

Too many Christians have become dangerously casual in the way they approach God. The modern trend is to view God more as our buddy than as an awe-inspiring, holy, and majestic God. Hebrews 12:28-29 says, "God is a consuming fire." The Bible is clear that the Lord is "sitting on a throne, high and lifted up" (Isaiah 6:1, NKJV).

It's all-too-human nature to want to reduce God to someone more like us, someone who's easy to understand and even easier to follow. But the Bible clearly says that's impossible: "For as the heavens are higher than the earth, so are My ways higher than your ways, and My thoughts than your thoughts" (Isaiah 55:9, NKJV). David wrote, "The Lord looked down from his sanctuary on high, from heaven he viewed the earth" (Psalm 102:19). We must never forget that enthroned God is still way up there looking way down *here* below. We can only worship God properly when we honor him as holy and far above any of us.

Let's pick up where we left off yesterday. With their enemies only about ten miles away and coming fast, Jehoshaphat and the people of Judah prayed to God for help. Jehoshaphat began his prayer by recognizing some unique things about God—what some call God's "transcendent" perfections because only God can possess them. There are parts of God's nature that we humans will never possess.

The first transcendent characteristic we see is God's *sovereignty*. That's a big word that means God is in charge. 🐦 Read 2 Chronicles 20:5-6. What might happen in your life if you truly believed these words about God are true?

No matter how much we try, no human can come up against almighty God and win. Pushing against God's plan is like trying to push the ocean waves back into the sea!

God is *sovereign* because he is also *all-powerful*. Jehoshaphat prayed, "Power and might are in your hand, and no one can withstand you" (2 Chronicles 20:6b). Jeremiah 32:17 says, "O Sovereign Lord! You made the heavens and earth by your strong hand and powerful arm. Nothing is too hard for you!" (NEW LIVING TRANSLATION).

One of my favorite biographies is Elisabeth Elliot's *Through Gates of Splendor*. It's the true story of five young men who answered God's call to take the gospel to a primitive tribe deep in the jungles of Ecuador. On their first attempt to meet the tribesmen, they were killed. Among them was Elisabeth Elliot's husband, Jim.[1]

Elisabeth Elliot wrote: "The quiet trust of the mothers helped the children to know that this was not a tragedy. This was what God had planned. To the world at large this was a sad waste of five young lives. But God has His plan and purpose in all things. There were those whose lives were changed by what happened."[2]

Situations like this will strip away people's head knowledge about God. It hits at the very core of us. So what was Elisabeth Elliot's secret? It was simply this: She saw everything that happened as the sovereign will of all-powerful God.

Jehoshaphat recognized one more thing about God that we can never emulate: He *never changes*. He's always the same. Jehoshaphat called God the "God of our fathers." That's another way of saying, "God, you're the *same* God our forefathers worshipped." And here's the best news: He's *still* the same today, still just as powerful and able to handle *our* problems and direct *our* lives.

Keep It Real

What is there about God that causes you to fear him, to respect and revere him? Lay those reasons out before God. Stop and thank God for being all-powerful and unchanging, yet loving and full of mercy. Then decide to "brag on Jesus" in the next twenty-four hours to your friends and family, which is another awesome way to praise him!

Keep It Pure

Do you try to reduce God to something you can understand and control? Change your perspective! Admit aloud God's mysterious and awesome power in your life today, and see what happens. Ask God to direct your every step and every word. Write your prayer below.

JOURNAL

Write this week's meditation verse, Philippians 3:10, below. Then invest a few minutes in memorizing it.

JOURNAL

---

[1] Elisabeth Elliot, *Through Gates of Splendor* (Wheaton, IL: Tyndale House Publishers, 1981), 252-253.
[2] Ibid., 271.

Yesterday we saw, very dimly, a supreme God up in the heavens. Today, our vision becomes clearer. We will come to see a loving God who left his high place and came down…all the way down to *us*! God's sovereign power brought the people of Judah great confidence, knowing God *could* help them. But it was God's relational qualities that brought his people great comfort and peace, because they knew their God *would* help them!

🐦 Read Jehoshaphat's prayer in 2 Chronicles 20:6-12. Imagine being in that scene. If you'd heard Jehoshaphat pray that prayer, would it have encouraged and comforted you? Why or why not?

There is one little word in this prayer that stands out more than any other. It connects God in heaven with people on earth. Because of this one word we can have hope and salvation. The word is *our*. That word shows the relationship God had with the people of Judah. He was their God, and they were his people. They needed more than "a god" or even "God"; they needed "*our* God" to come and save them.

The people of Judah had at least three good reasons to know he was their God. The first reason is God's *faithfulness*. Every promise God ever made with his people has been kept. Jehoshaphat reminded the Lord of one of those promises when he said, "Did you not drive out the inhabitants of this land before your people Israel and give it forever to the descendants of Abraham?" (verse 7). It's always a healthy practice to remember how God has come through for us in the past.

What's hard to believe is that God remains faithful to *us* even when we're not faithful to *him*. That's because of his *relationship* with us. It's the relationship of a loving father with his child—completely permanent, thoroughly dependable.

When Jehoshaphat appointed singers, he mentioned another of God's relational qualities. He instructed them to praise God "for the splendor of His holiness" (verse 21). People often think of holiness as some weird separation from reality (and from any possibility of fun!). The word conjures up images of people dressed in black, carrying ten-pound Bibles and jumping out of corners yelling,

"Repent!" But being holy doesn't mean to act strangely. It *does* mean we're to stay away from sin and be set apart for Jesus.

God's goal for our lives is *holiness*, and that's another great reason to know we belong to him. Leviticus 11:45 says, "Be holy, because I am holy." Some Christians would rather ignore the Lord's command to be holy. Sure, it's great to lean on God's faithfulness. But if we can think we can act any way we want and still receive his blessings and protection, we are terribly misguided. God loves us, and he is determined to make us more like his Son (Romans 8:29).

We have one more incredible reason to know he is *our* God who loves us. Simply put, God's mercy endures forever. Mercy is the holding back of God's judgment. We've all sinned and fallen short of God's glory (Romans 3:23). We all deserve to be in hell forever, separated from God. Yet God doesn't treat us as our sins deserve. He forgives anyone who turns to him for *enduring mercy*.

Our God has come down to us through Jesus. No wonder Paul practically shouted it off the page, "Thank God for this gift [his Son] too wonderful for words!" (2 Corinthians 9:15, NLT).

Keep It Real

Try this: Go through these relational qualities of God, and journal what comes to mind.

1) Think for a minute about how *faithful* God is to you, of how he always keeps his promises. Write down what comes to mind.

JOURNAL

2) Now consider how *holy* and perfect God is. Do you see ways you fall short of being perfect like him? Write them down.

3) Now thank God for the *mercy* he faithfully shows you. Say *out loud* how glad you are that God is making you more like Jesus every day. Put this on paper, too.

Keep It Pure

If you've never placed your faith and trust in Jesus as your Savior, pray this prayer now: "Dear Jesus, I know I've sinned. I know you died on the cross for my sins and that you came back to life. Please forgive me now. I trust you as my Savior and my Lord. I give you my life. Save me right now. Thank you for saving me because I asked. Thank you."

If you prayed that prayer, please tell your parents or someone at church who can encourage you in your new faith in Jesus! Don't wait. Tell someone *now*.

Personal God

To know God in a personal way is to deeply understand the meaning of one of Jesus' names, Immanuel. *Immanuel* means "God with us." Not only is Jesus "God with us"—he can and should be God with *me*. That's God's ultimate goal—to be a very intimate God with each of us.

It's sad to say, but true friendship with the Lord is rare these days. You might be surprised to hear that this is often true even among worship leaders and Christian musicians. You'd think they know him well because they sing and play for God so often. But one doesn't necessarily lead to the other.

Here's another example: How can a person constantly look into space and not be completely humbled and awestruck? Yet astronomers who make their living looking at stars sometimes fail to see just how awesome those stars really are.

Likewise, those who play and sing in a worship band are in danger of merely going through the motions of "professional praise." They may sing *toward* God, but the questions they need to ask themselves are these: Do we sing *to* God? Do we love to tell him how awesome he is?

It's not just musicians. Many church people never connect on an intimate level with the very One to whom they're singing. That's why friendship with a personal God is so very important—in fact, it's an absolute must—for all Christians.

No doubt someone out there is thinking something like this: But how can we know for sure that God *wants* to be that personal to us? Isn't it enough that he knows my name among so many billions of Christians? Now you say he wants to get involved with every detail of my life—where I go to school, who I hang out with, who I'm friends with on Facebook. So if I stub my toe, you mean he actually *wants* to know and help?

The answer is *yes*! God wants to be a part of every area of your life! Matthew 10:29 teaches that the Lord even cares when a sparrow falls. Imagine how much more he watches over us!

In 2 Chronicles 20:7, Jehoshaphat called Abraham God's friend because God himself said Abraham was his friend (Isaiah 41:8). I imagine Jehoshaphat was also hoping that God would be *their* friend that day as those armies marched against them. They sure needed one!

Who better to teach us about friendship than Jesus? He had many friends! He was even called a friend of sinners (Luke 7:34). There are at least three lessons we can learn from Jesus about friendship with holy God.

Read John 15:13-16. As you read, remember that Jesus is talking to his disciples only a few days before his crucifixion.

The first thing we learn here is that *Christ chooses us* (verse 16). God *initiates* the friendship with us. J.I. Packer wrote, "*We* do not make friends with *God*; *God* makes friends with *us*, bringing us to know him by making His love known to us."[1]

The second insight from Jesus' life is that *some friendships with God are closer than others*. I don't mean some people get more cozy with God than others, that some might get off the hook with God for certain things while others won't. No, we will all stand before the impartial Judge one day and give an account of our lives (1 Peter 1:17). But Jesus was closer to those he *trusted* the most. Because the disciples were his trusted friends, he told them things he couldn't tell anyone else.

One final lesson for us from Jesus' friendships is this: To be God's friend, we must do what he tells us to do and *prove* ourselves trustworthy. We just saw that there was certain information Jesus could only give to those he knew were his friends. It's important to note that Judas wasn't there at that point. He had already run out to betray Jesus. Judas didn't get in on Jesus' confidential bit of info. Judas wasn't Jesus' friend because he couldn't be *trusted*.

Keep It Real

Pray a prayer *out loud* now praising God that he is the fearful and powerful One. Then, thank him that he is also the God who wants to be your friend. Write your prayer below, if you like.

JOURNAL

Draw a circle in the margin of this book or in your personal journal. Then draw a small chair right in the center of the circle. The circle represents your heart, the innermost part of you. The chair symbolizes the throne inside your heart. Where is God right now? Can you say that he's sitting on the throne of your heart? Or, are you seated there instead? Place an X where God is in your heart and in regard to your will.

Jesus said, "You are my friends if you do whatever I command you" (John 15:14, NKJV). Ask God what you need to do to be a more trusted friend to him. Willingly submit now to whatever God's telling you to do. Stay in prayer until you can honestly say God is seated on your heart's throne.

JOURNAL

[1] J.I. Packer, *Knowing God* (Downers Grove, IL: Intervarsity Press, 1973), 4.

PURE PRAISE
FOR YOUTH

By-Products of Knowing God

Meeting someone for the first time doesn't mean we really *know* that person. Likewise, when we first trusted Jesus as our Savior, we met him. But, to get to *know* Jesus well, we invest time with him and focus on him. The amazing news is that Jesus *wants* us to know him!

To be true worshippers, we must have a hunger to know our God. Like David, our prayer should be: "As a deer longs for flowing streams, so my soul longs for You, O God. My soul thirsts for God, for the living God. When shall I come and behold the face of God?" (Psalm 42:1-2, Revised Standard Version).

As we get to know God through investing time with him and worshipping him, we discover there are several benefits that come with the investment. Granted, we should worship the Lord simply because he demands, desires, and deserves it. But it's also true that we can never out-give God! The more we give him worship, the more undeserved blessings he piles on us, way beyond our imaginations! Just try to wrap your mind and heart around a few of the many perks of knowing God.

To start with, the more we get to know God, the more *he develops our character*. That's our moral fiber and personality. We always become what we worship. If we focus on the world or other individuals we tend to become like them. If we focus on God, we'll become more like him.

Read Paul's words in 2 Corinthians 3:18. What do you think it means to be changed into God's image?

A great way to summarize that verse is this: *Gaze upon God and be transformed*. As Dan DeHaan puts it, "Find me a worshiper of God, and I will show you a stable man with his mind in control, ready to meet the present hour with refreshment from above." [1]

Another result of knowing God is *freedom from intimidation*. We are to be rooted and built up in Christ (Colossians 2:6-10). Because we are complete in Christ, we should not in any way be intimidated by "super saints." There will always be people who know more about the Bible than you or I know. There will always be people with more faith in God than we have. But Jesus is the only standard you or I must compare ourselves to. When we are in his will, doing what he wants us to do, we can be confident that God is pleased with us just the way we are.

A third benefit of knowing God is *concern for people who don't know Jesus*. We no longer have to "work up" a burden for our friends or neighbors who don't know Jesus. As we realize God's heart for them, his burden for their salvation will become our burden! After all, who has a greater desire to see this world trust in

Jesus than his Father? He gave up his Son to make that happen. God must care a lot to do that. I want and need his passion for those who don't know Jesus burning in my soul. So I must get to know him *better*.

Getting to know God and waiting before him also brings *energy in serving the Lord*. Isaiah 40:30-31 says, "Even the youths shall faint and be weary, and the young men shall utterly fall, but those who wait on the Lord shall renew their strength; they shall mount up with wings like eagles, they shall run and not be weary, they shall walk and not faint" (NKJV).

True satisfaction in God is yet another amazing perk that comes from knowing God well. Complete satisfaction is rare. Too often people depend on their successes or other people's opinions to make them happy and fulfilled. They base their contentment on some source other than God. But none of us will ever be truly content until we come to God's table to be filled. Jesus said, "You're blessed when you've worked up a good appetite for God. He's food and drink in the best meal you'll ever eat" (Matthew 5:6, THE MESSAGE). Once we've feasted on the Bread of Life, nothing else looks nearly as tempting.

Keep It Real

Choose one or two of the benefits we studied today. Write a prayer of thanksgiving to God for giving you such blessings and the opportunity to know him more and more.

JOURNAL

PURE PRAISE
FOR YOUTH

Quote this week's meditation verse, Philippians 3:10. Look it up in your Bible if you're not sure. Now write a prayer committing yourself to knowing God at all costs.

[1]Dan DeHaan, *The God You Can Know* (Chicago, IL: Moody Press, 1982), 17.

For this session, you'll need:

• 1 magazine for every 2 people in your group

Leader: Select magazines with information about celebrities, athletes, or other well-known people. You might opt for a different group of magazine titles based on whether you lead a girls' group or a guys' group.

GET CONNECTED (15 minutes)

It's great to have everyone here today. I'm sure each of you knows all kinds of information about your favorite athletes, celebrities, musicians, or other famous people. We're going to all learn from you in just a moment. First, select a person in the group to be your partner for this activity.

Allow people to form pairs. It's OK to have one trio if needed. Distribute one magazine to each pair.

Here are your instructions: Look through your magazine together and choose one person who is featured somewhere in the magazine. Using the information you find in the magazine, you'll report to the rest of our group on that particular person. If you already know other bits of trivia or information about this person, you'll be able to share that with us, too. You'll have about three minutes to read and prepare, so work quickly.

Give pairs three minutes to read and discuss, and then bring everyone back together. Give each pair about a minute to share details about the famous person they "researched." Then discuss these questions: → → 1

It's great to know lots of things *about* people, but it's more meaningful when we actually *know* people. When we read the Bible, we learn a lot *about* God, but God doesn't want us to stop there. Part of the adventure of leading a lifestyle of worship is genuinely *knowing* God—what matters to God, what God values, how much God loves you, and the specific plans and desires God has for your life.

DIG DEEPER (25 minutes)

Most of you probably know about a man in the Old Testament named Abraham. But you may not know that he's mentioned in the New Testament in a unique way. Let's look at that now. Can someone read James 2:23?

After your volunteer reads, discuss these questions: → → 2

PURE PRAISE
FOR YOUTH

→ → **1**
- So, clearly, all of you know a lot of things about these individuals—but how well do you really *know* the people themselves? Explain.
- Think about one of your friends. What steps or actions took you from just knowing *about* that person to actually *knowing* that person?

 JAMES 2:23

→ → **2**
- What do you think it means to be God's friend?

- How is a friendship with God similar to or different from your other friendships?

- Think of the ways you build friendships with others. Which of those habits, choices, attitudes, or actions carries over into your pursuit of a deep friendship with God? What looks different?

This week's meditation verse is Philippians 3:10. Who'd like to read that verse for us? → →3

BRING IT TO LIFE (20 minutes)

As we learned from Dwayne this week, a great relationship—especially one with God—isn't just about hanging out and having a good time. So let's dig a little deeper here. Can someone read James 1:22-25? → →4

We've talked today about the importance of knowing God, developing a friend-ship with God, and obeying what God reveals in the Bible. Right now, I'd like you to do something you'd normally never do during our group time: Pull out your cell phones and text someone. Seriously! Text someone who isn't in the room right now; share a word of encouragement or support or love. Take a few seconds to think of the person you want to text, and then take up to two minutes to write your message. If you can send words of friendship to more than one person in the next two minutes, go for it.

If group members don't have cell phones with them, ask them to write the name of a friend and a sentence stating why that person is so valued and significant. Encourage those writing this way to pass along these messages to their friends in an e-mail, a text message, a card, or during their next conversation.

After two minutes, regain everyone's attention.

Building friendships—including our friendship with God—requires effort and commitment and action. Let's ask God to help us to take the next steps in building those relationships.

Pray that each person in the group would develop a deeper friendship with God and would discover how to truly *know* God in richer, clearer ways.

PHILIPPIANS 3:10

→ → **3** • What do you think it means to experience the power that raised Jesus from the dead—*and* to share in his suffering?

• How would each of those experiences help you know Jesus more deeply? Give examples if you can.

• Does this verse inspire you or scare you? Why?

JAMES 1:22-25

→ → **4** • What reasons does James give for obeying what's in the Bible, instead of just reading or knowing what's there? What other reasons can you think of?

• When have you been obedient to God even when it hurt? How has that helped deepen your relationship with God?

HEARING GOD

DAY 1

Our Most Needed Ability

This week's goal is for you to become more aware of God's presence every moment of every day. Each day, you'll practice listening for God's gentle whisper. So let's get started.

The first question I want to help you answer today is whether you *can* actually hear from God. Do you really have what it takes to listen to his voice? An even bigger question, then, is this: *Does* God still speak today? After all, you can't hear what's not being said.

The answer is absolutely *yes*! God *definitely* still speaks today!

There are tons of ways people stay connected with their friends these days—Facebook, Twitter, Skype, texting (*lots* of texting!), talking on cell phones. And of course, old-fashioned face-to-face communication never goes out of style. God also has a variety of ways he talks with us, but there are four primary ways we'll touch upon today.

First of all, God speaks through his *Word*, the Bible. Joshua 1:8-9 says that God promises to prosper and direct us when we meditate on the Book of the Law day and night and are careful to do everything written in it. Paul likewise urged Timothy to listen to God through his Word: "All Scripture is inspired by God and is useful to teach us what is true and to make us realize what is wrong in our lives. It corrects us when we are wrong and teaches us to do what is right. God uses it to prepare and equip his people to do every good work" (2 Timothy 3:16-17, New Living Translation). The Bible is also the authority on all the other ways God might choose to communicate. That's why it's so important to read it every day!

God also speaks to us through *other Christians*. Proverbs 11:14 tells us that with many counselors, there is safety. The Lord often uses friends and adults to encourage and counsel us, and sometimes even to give us needed correction.

A third way God communicates with us is through our *circumstances*. As someone wisely said, "Circumstances drive us to our knees so the only way we can look is up!" The three armies coming to attack Jerusalem in 2 Chronicles 20 were certainly enough to drive the people of Judah to their knees in prayer.

Of course, the circumstances God uses to speak to us aren't always bad. One of the reasons the Lord brings good things into people's lives is to get their attention. Paul said, "Don't you see how wonderfully kind, tolerant, and patient God is with you? Does this mean nothing to you? Can't you see that his kindness is intended to turn you from your sin?" (Romans 2:4, NLT).

One other channel through which the Lord speaks today—and one present in all the other channels here—is the Holy Spirit. Paul said the Spirit was his source of instruction: "This is what we speak, not in words taught us by human wisdom but in words taught by the Spirit, expressing spiritual truths in spiritual words" (1 Corinthians 2:13).

Conditions for Hearing

So now that we know God still speaks today, let's come back to our first question: Can you hear God speak? Again, the answer is yes! No matter where you are in life—even if you don't have a relationship with Jesus—you can hear him as he draws you to him. God can break through even the hardest heart and reveal himself to individuals.

However, for God to lead us and guide us each day with his still small voice, there are certain conditions we must meet. In John chapter 10, Jesus showed exactly how we can all hear Jesus when he calls.

First, we must *know* Jesus. We have to be in the sheepfold. Read John 10:3-11 in your Bible. If you've trusted Jesus as your Savior, the day you became a Christian is the day *you* became a sheep, and you developed spiritual ears that could hear his voice!

To consistently hear from God, though, it's not enough just to have ears. Those ears must be *sensitive* to his voice. The last part of verse 4 says, "His sheep follow him because they know his voice." The sheep know his voice because they've heard it before. They've learned to recognize it. The more you listen to the Lord, the more you recognize his soft, gentle voice.

But even with ears to listen, it's possible to miss God's voice. That's because there's one final condition: You must give yourself over to God, or be *surrendered* to him. The idea here is not only to have open, sensitive ears, but to have ears that are bent *toward* God, *wanting* to receive his instructions. This should be your attitude: Lord, counsel me, correct me, teach me, direct me, rebuke me… just please *talk* to me!

Being able to hear from the Lord should be at the top of the priority list for everyone who worships and follows him. The reason is simple: *If we don't hear from the Lord, we don't know what to do.* The Lord is our leader, our shepherd. We are dumb sheep who need to be led. However, being led means laying down our pride and self-will.

Can you imagine the shepherd standing up in front of the herd and discussing his plans with the sheep? "Sheep, let me have your attention. Today we're going to the south forty to graze. Now, before you get all bent out of shape, let me explain to you *why* we're going to the south forty..." Ridiculous, isn't it? Our job as sheep isn't to try to understand everything the Shepherd does. Our job simply is to *follow* wherever he leads us.

A friend once said to me, "I've been asking God for direction, but he hasn't given me any. I hope he's not going to lead me to be a preacher because that's one thing I'm not willing to do! Why won't he just tell me what I'm supposed to do?"

With that attitude, I seriously doubt my friend ever got an answer! If we aren't willing to obey God's voice, why should he bother talking to us? Like Samuel, we need to surrender and say, "Speak, for your servant is listening" (1 Samuel 3:10b).

Keep It Real

When was the last time you took a few moments to really look at a sunset or a night sky?

Take a moment now and describe how it looked, the colors you saw, the size and shapes of the clouds, and the position of the sun.

JOURNAL

Decide to stop and notice today's sunset if you can. Deliberately praise God for designing it. Become more sensitive to God's presence around you.

The meditation verse for this week is Isaiah 50:4, and it's a great verse about listening to God. Write it below.

Listen now for God's voice. Obey whatever God is telling you at this moment. Write down what you think God might be saying to you.

A Crisis Mindset

When most people hear the word *crisis*, they think of running around, biting their fingernails, and being filled with worry and stress. But when the people of Judah found themselves in the crisis of 2 Chronicles 20, that wasn't their response. When they heard about the armies marching toward them, they didn't fall to pieces. Instead, their potential disaster drove them to seek God's help. Their crisis actually catapulted them *toward* what God needed them to know to overcome their situation.

Jehoshaphat and the people of Judah had what I like to call a "crisis mindset." A crisis mindset has a simple definition: *We've got a problem, and only God can solve it.* People who have this crisis mindset are rare, but they're fairly easy to spot. They have three unique characteristics.

First, people who have this mindset are *desperate* to hear from God. Jehoshaphat knew his people were powerless against the vast army coming against them. In the same way, our own feeble strength is no match for our enemy, the devil. Satan hates it when we worship God from our hearts; to deny or ignore Satan's attempts to interfere in our lives is both foolish and dangerous. We must have the help of our God, who is greater in us "than he who is in the world" (1 John 4:4, New King James Version).

Jehoshaphat recognized he simply wasn't smart enough to make the right decision in this situation. He needed God's help. Those of us who help lead others at church or in our youth groups could learn a great lesson here. Too often we depend on our talents, experience, and human logic to carry us week after week. We begin to think we don't really need to pray that much. If we have a crisis—a problem we can't handle on our own—*then* we'll pray hard.

But that's exactly the point: We *always* have a crisis before us. We're in spiritual battle with the powers of darkness *every day*! Our own smarts are grossly inadequate; we've got to have the Lord's constant direction.

I believe Jehoshaphat felt most desperate when he thought about his people. No doubt they were shaking with fear. What could he possibly do that could give them hope and help? The answer: He could, and did, let them hear from God.

🕊 Stop now and think about the people in church with you each week. Who could be in crisis right now? Pray specifically for those people this week. Ask God to give you a portion of their burdens, to allow you to share in their crises. Write down the names that came to mind.

As important as it is to recognize that we're desperate, desperation alone isn't enough. We must also be *determined* to hear from God. Jehoshaphat, when he got the frightening news, "resolved to inquire of the Lord." The people of Judah *needed* to hear from God, so they committed themselves to God. Jehoshaphat "proclaimed a fast for all Judah" so that the entire nation would completely yield themselves to the Lord. They confessed their need for God as they sought his help.

🕊 Read 2 Chronicles 20:12-13. When have you made a similar admission to God, and how did God respond?

I remember a little habit I tried to maintain when I was in high school. In the minutes just before I walked into school each day, I said a simple, quiet "breath prayer" confessing how much I needed the Lord to help me live for him in front of my friends.

Still to this day, anytime I'm about to speak or sing to a group of people, I try to find an empty room or a corner where I can be alone. There, I kneel before God and ask him to speak and sing through me. It's one of the most powerfully refreshing practices I've ever experienced.

Once the people of Judah confessed their great need for God, they waited before God. They concentrated on God; their eyes were fixed on him. They weren't going to budge from that spot until God told them what to do. It wasn't a matter of *if* God would speak to them, but *when*.

How long they stood there waiting, we don't know. It doesn't really matter. What matters is that they *decided* they were going to get an answer from God about their crisis. And they stood there until they did.

Deciding we *will* hear from God is the third characteristic of a "crisis mindset." And like the people of Judah, when God speaks to us and shows us what he wants us to do, our feeling of crisis turns to total *confidence*! Then we know that the battle is God's, not ours. All we really have to do is "stand firm and see the deliverance the Lord will give you" (2 Chronicles 20:17).

Keep It Real

Think about a difficult situation you or someone you know is in right now. What does the Bible have to say about that situation? Get *desperate, determined,* and *decided* about it. Thank God that he'll do what he says he'll do. Praise God for his Word! Write a prayer stating your trust in God.

JOURNAL

Keep It Pure

Ask God to show you ways you're depending on yourself and your own abilities rather than looking to him for strength and direction. Express your *desperation* for God as you go through your day today. Let God know you are *determined* to listen to whatever he wants to tell you. Then *decide* to wait for God's answer.

JOURNAL

PURE PRAISE
FOR YOUTH

So far this week, we've learned that God can and must be heard by us—his sheep. But what does his voice *sound* like? How can we know when it's *God* who's speaking to us?

I once knew a teenager named Phillip who'd been involved in our youth group for about a year. One day while we were riding down the road, Phillip turned to me and said, "You're always saying that God spoke to you; God said this or God said that to you. But I don't understand. I can't tell when God's talking to me. How can you be so sure?" Phillip's question was a wake-up call. I'd been working with him, trying to disciple him for months, yet I'd never taken time to explain one of the most basic activities of the Christian life: *recognizing God's voice!*

I'll never forget my mom's distinctive voice when she would call me to come inside from playing. Even if I was several houses away, that high-pitched yell— "Dwaaayne! Come to supper!"—pierced the air and got my attention. But how did I know that it was my mom's voice? There were four things that assured me that the voice in the distance was, in fact, my mom's.

First of all, my mom's voice was *familiar*. I'd heard it many times before. No one else's voice sounded quite like that, so it was easy for me to recognize.

Read John 10:3-5. How are you like or unlike the sheep in this example?

The sheep have heard the shepherd's voice before, and they've learned to recognize it. Even a newborn baby will turn his head and eyes toward his mother when she speaks because he'd heard her voice so often before he was born.

Not only was my mom's voice (and the Shepherd's voice) familiar, it was also *personal*. She clearly said my name—Dwayne. When God speaks to us, he wants us to know exactly who he's talking to. So he calls us by name.

Thirdly, my mother's voice was easy to recognize because it was *simple and clear*. What if she had said, "Dwayne, I implore thee to make haste and move in the general direction of thine homestead with the express purpose of finding sustenance and renewed energy for thy body"? I'm sure I would have said, "Do *what*?"

I'm thankful that God puts his words in a language each of us can understand! I mean, how much more *simple* can one get than Jesus' words in John 10: 9, "I am the gate"? Everyone knows what a gate is. Anyone should get the idea.

There was something else about my mom's voice that I could always count on: It was *full of love*. I knew whatever she said came from a heart that cared deeply for me. Even when she raised her voice because she was upset with me, her words corrected me and made me better. Listen to the love in Jesus' words:

"I have come that they may have life, and have it to the full. I am the good shepherd. The good shepherd lays down his life for the sheep" (John 10:10b-11).

Many of us continue to walk around, feeling guilty and condemned for sins we've already confessed to God. Despite our attempts to believe God has forgiven us (like he promised he would), something inside keeps bringing those sins and shortcomings back to our minds, pushing us down even further.

That something is actually someone: Satan, the "accuser of our brethren" (Revelation 12:10, NKJV), who seeks to condemn us with his words. The Lord, by contrast, will never speak to us to condemn us. He wants only for us to have his abundant life. Even when God's correcting us, his purpose is still ultimately to make us more like his Son.

I've always loved Philippians 3:14. Paul said, "I press on toward the goal to win the prize for which God has called me heavenward in Christ Jesus." But for a long time, I would stop there. I never really noticed verse 15, "All of us who are mature should take such a view of things. And if on some point you think differently, that too God will make clear to you."

Did you catch that? "That too God will make clear to you." That means if you and I are determined to please God and press forward, there's no way God will allow us to make a mistake or misunderstand his leading! We *will* hear and know God's voice! He will make absolutely sure of it! God loves his children so much that he won't let us go off course! What an awesome God we serve!

Keep It Real

Take some time now to brag on the Lord! Tell him what you love about him. Since it's God's praise you're giving back to him, why not ask God to *help* you praise him? Pray as David prayed, "O Lord, open my lips, and my mouth will declare your praise" (Psalm 51:15). Journal some of the things you said to God as you praised him.

JOURNAL

Write out the meditation verse, Isaiah 50:4. Read it through several times, thinking about every word and what the verse means.

Keep It Pure

Are you really determined to live for Jesus every day? Are you "pressing toward" being more like him? Ask Jesus to show you any areas in your life where you haven't given him full control.

Fine-Tuning Our Ears

I'm grateful that God will find a way to speak to us as we live for him. But how far must God go to get our attention? Will it require some difficult situation or traumatic experience? I've heard people say, "I guess I just had to learn the hard way." But *did* they? Could the problem have been avoided if they'd listened more closely to start with—or even more likely, obeyed what they'd heard? There's a good chance the Shepherd warned them about that ditch before they ever had a chance to fall into it.

That's why it's not enough to have ears that *eventually* hear God's voice. We must have ears that can *easily* hear his voice and respond to it.

Read 2 Chronicles 20:12-17 now. How do you think Jahaziel knew what to say?

Listening ability like Jahaziel's did not come naturally. He had to train, or fine-tune, his spiritual ears. In the same way, if we're to hear the Lord's voice more easily, there are three important things we must do.

First, we must *practice listening*. That seems obvious, yet how much effort do we actually put into really listening for God's voice each day? How many mornings do we awake ready to listen in case God wants to speak to us? How often do we lie awake at night thinking about him?

Think back over your day yesterday. How many times did you stop to listen for God or ask him to speak to you? Was it once, twice, ten times…*no* times? It's still true: Practice makes perfect—or at least better. We can't expect to learn to better recognize God's voice if we're not constantly listening.

People seem to think that prophets in the Bible had some kind of extra-tall spiritual antenna that made it easier for them to pick up a clear signal! But even prophets had to learn to recognize God's voice. Samuel was one of the greatest prophets in the Old Testament. However, when God first called Samuel by name, Samuel thought it was the priest Eli speaking to him. Samuel heard a voice, but couldn't tell whose it was. That would take both time and practice to learn. Like Samuel, every day we should say to God, "Speak, for your servant is listening" (1 Samuel 3:10).

A word of caution: Take as much time as you need to be sure you're hearing God's voice. Make sure it's *familiar, personal, simple and clear*, and *loving*. God will wait for you. Satan wants to deceive and confuse you about whose voice you're hearing. But if you take the time to be sure it's God's voice, over time you'll more readily recognize and respond whenever God speaks to your heart.

A second thing we must do to more easily hear from God is *focus our thoughts*. Some guitarists like to tune their guitars "by ear." Rather than using an electronic tuner, they rely on their ears to tell them when each string is in tune. This, of course, requires total concentration on the notes they're playing.

Jehoshaphat and the people of Judah obviously understood the need to concentrate in order to hear from God. They focused their minds totally toward him. That is what Jehoshaphat meant when he said, "Our eyes are upon you" (2 Chronicles 20:12b).

Try concentrating on the Lord like they did. Take one full minute to think only thoughts about God. Don't allow any other thoughts to clutter your mind. Focus completely on him. Ready, get set, think!

So how did you do? It wasn't easy, was it? I admit, the first time I tried that little exercise I didn't do well at all! I was amazed by how many other thoughts battled for my attention.

Second Chronicles 10:5 says that we're to "take captive every thought to make it obedient to Christ." Notice that this passage does *not* say that every thought we have will immediately reflect Jesus. That's impossible, since Satan sometimes shoots evil thoughts into our minds. But as soon as a thought enters our minds, it must be seized and checked. If it honors God, it stays. If that thought might dishonor the Lord, throw it out, *now*.

To more easily hear God's voice, there's one more thing we must do. We must *respond* every time the Lord speaks to us. As we respond to each prompting from God, we'll sensitize our spiritual ears to his voice, and learn to recognize even the gentlest whisper from the Spirit.

Keep It Real

Kneel where you are right now. Hold up your hands before God as though you're saying "I surrender." Then, in your heart, actually surrender to whatever God leads you to do today. As you kneel with your hands raised, sing a song to God. It's just you and God, and he loves to hear you sing—no matter *what* your voice sounds like! Remember, he *made* your voice!

Keep It Pure

Pray now. Ask God to fine-tune your ears to hear his voice today. Promise to respond with obedience and/or deliberate praise. Journal your prayer.

JOURNAL

Expecting to Hear

We've invested this week in learning how and why to listen to God. Today's session, therefore, is reserved for doing what we've talked about. So let's take some time today to quiet ourselves and just listen. Deliberately slow your pace down as you read this page.

First, read Psalm 46:10 in your Bible. Then read it again—more slowly and thoughtfully.

When Jesus was in the wilderness for forty days (Luke 4), I'm sure he did a lot of *listening*, too. Follow Jesus' example now. Stop your reading. Be still and listen. Again, take your time here. What do you sense God might be saying to you through the verse you just read? Write down any thoughts that come to mind right now.

JOURNAL

Now talk to God. But don't say too much. In just a sentence or two, ask God to reveal himself to you today. Tell God something you're thankful for. Give him a brief statement of praise. But that's all. Now go back to listening closely...

Now confess any known sins God brings to your mind. Speak them. Resolve to turn away from them. Then listen some more...

As you're hopefully already noticing, prayer is communicating with God in both directions. He talks; we listen. We talk; he listens. At this moment the priority is *us* listening to *God* speak. Like Jesus, decide to only "say whatever the Father tells [you] to say" (John 12:50, NLT). So take at least a few more moments to listen before moving on.

Jehoshaphat and the people of Judah in 2 Chronicles 20 put themselves in a position to hear from God. That's also what Jesus did. Jesus would rise early to invest time alone with his Father. W. Phillip Keller said, "The biographies of great men and women of God repeatedly point out how the secret of the success in their spiritual life was attributed to the 'quiet time' of each morning." [1]

Our goal is not just to have a "quiet time" that we can check off our list of things to do. Our goal today, and every day, is to connect with Almighty God. We must wait before God until we've given him every opportunity to speak.

Don't think that these five days complete our training in hearing God's voice. Our education has just begun. In fact, in the "art of listening school," we're *all* freshmen! School's still in session, and we must *never* stop learning how to listen.

Prioritizing Time With God

As a fifteen-year-old, I was sitting in a church service about to do a concert. Just minutes before I was to begin, the Spirit of the Lord spoke strongly to my own spirit, "Dwayne, I will not help you today as you sing if you do not commit to get up every morning for the rest of your life and spend time alone with me."

Talk about blowing a kid's mind! I had to go outside right then and talk it out with God. "Lord, I'm only fifteen! I'm not sure I'm ready to make such a big vow. Can't I maybe wait a few years before I lock myself into this?" "Not if you want to be anointed," was the reply. "But I can't sing—or *live*, for that matter—without your hand on me!" God said, "Then decide right now to make time for me every day from this day on."

When I said yes, and began the regular discipline of placing myself before the Lord to hear daily from him, my spiritual growth skyrocketed!

I share this personal story because I want you to see how important *God* considers *your* time alone with him. How God leads you might well be different from how he led me, but one thing's for sure: God wants to be with *all* of us, *regularly*.

Keep It Real

Praise God *out loud* for speaking to you today. What a privilege that God would care enough for us to even take time for us! Thank God in advance for how he may prompt you today to help someone else or share your faith with a person who needs to know his hope. Write a prayer of praise.

JOURNAL

Keep It Pure

Say this week's meditation verse, Isaiah 50:4. Do it from memory if possible. Now say it again as a prayer to God.

Bow your knees (if you're physically able). Bow your mind, your emotions, and your heart before the Lord. Listen quietly, attentively. What is God telling you that you haven't written down yet? Write it now.

JOURNAL

[1]W. Phillip Keller, *A Shepherd Looks at Psalm 23* (Grand Rapids, MI: Zondervan, 2007), 61.

For this session, you'll need:

- Notecards
- Pens or pencils

GET CONNECTED (15 minutes)

Let's start today by practicing something most of us don't do often: speaking quietly! But first, we're going to put a little distance between each of us. Find a place to stand, but try to get as far away from everyone else as possible.

Give everyone time to find a spot in your meeting area. If you have a large group, count out groups of six for this activity. Give everyone notecards and pens or pencils.

I'm going to start by saying something very quietly about myself to the whole group—you'll probably have a tough time hearing me. I might whisper what I ate for lunch today, or the last movie I watched, or the last person I read about in the Bible. Write down on your notecard what you heard me say—or what you *think* you heard me say. Then the person to my left will whisper something to the whole group; write it down, too. We'll go around the room so everyone will get a chance.

After everyone has whispered, take turns revealing what each person said, in the order you originally went. Applaud the person who did the best job of hearing. Then discuss these questions: → → 1

This week, we've been learning about the importance of hearing God. As we continue in the journey of leading a lifestyle of worship, we need to remain in tune with what God's saying and revealing to us. Let's learn some more.

DIG DEEPER (25 minutes)

Form groups of four. Have a volunteer read 1 Samuel 3:1-18, and then spend ten minutes discussing these questions: → → 2

Bring everyone back together after about ten minutes. Share highlights and insights from your discussion time.

I'd like a volunteer to read this week's meditation verse, Isaiah 50:4. → → 3

→ → **1**
- What was the biggest challenge for you in this activity?
- What are some of the distractions, noises, and "static" that make it difficult to hear what *God's* trying to tell you? Or does it just seem as if God's not talking loudly enough? Explain.

 1 SAMUEL 3:1-18

→ → **2**
- How did Samuel (and Eli, for that matter) figure out whether it was really God who was speaking?

- Talk about a time you responded to God's leading or voice or direction. What was the result of your obedience?

 ISAIAH 50:4

→ → **3**
- How have you grown in your understanding of God's will and his plans for your life? How do you most want to continue growing?

- Why do we sometimes think that we don't need God's help—that we can do it all on our own?

For the next three minutes, I want you to do nothing but sit still. Don't pray. Don't talk. Don't read. Just sit still and listen. God may reveal something to you during these three minutes, or God may not. I simply want each of you to practice the habit of being still and listening for God's leading.

Regain everyone's attention after three minutes. Ask for volunteers to share insights they gained from this time of silence

BRING IT TO LIFE (15 minutes)

The Bible sometimes compares us to sheep—maybe it's not the most flattering comparison but it's an accurate one. Let's look at one passage that explains the importance of recognizing the voice of the Shepherd.

Read John 10:3-11, and then discuss these questions: → → 4

Find a partner, and take five minutes to discuss these questions together. I'll close us in prayer afterward. → → 5

After five minutes, regain everyone's attention. Pray for the group, asking God to help your students grow in their relationship with him and develop their awareness of his voice and leading in their lives.

PURE PRAISE
FOR YOUTH

JOHN 10:3-11

→ → **4** • What's your reaction to the idea of hearing and recognizing God's voice? Do you think you can hear Jesus that clearly? Explain.

• What's the difference between having a "quiet time" with God on your daily checklist and really taking the time to hear God every day? What does it look like, in both cases?

→ → **5** • What's an issue you're facing right now that only God can solve? How difficult is it for you to *let* God solve it? Explain.

• How might God use this situation to help you grow in your faith and trust in him? What are some real-life, practical steps you can take to become more sensitive to God's voice and leading?

WORSHIPPING WITH OTHERS

DAY 1

It's Not About Style

In order to set the tone for this week, I want to share a very personal and less-than-flattering story.

A few years ago in Gatlinburg, Tennessee, I visited a small country church one Wednesday night. I couldn't help but notice that the sanctuary was packed with people—for a church business meeting, no less! Fortunately, the business portion only lasted another ten minutes. Then a guy who I assumed was their worship leader stood up with a hymn book, and he asked for some singers to "come on up and help" him.

"Oh no," I thought, "it's been *years* since I've seen anyone do it like this." You see, growing up, I'd seen this "y'all come" approach to leading songs many times. It used to be fairly common among some of the small, country churches to ask several people—often unskilled and unrehearsed—to line up across the front and help lead. I was dreading it already.

They called out the number of their first hymn, a song no doubt written way before my time. "Yep, just as I suspected," my inner dialogue continued to sneer. "Their song selection is following right in line with their leadership style—old and outdated. Obviously these people are out of touch with how we do praise and worship nowadays. Somebody needs to enlighten them to some of the new stuff that's out there."

The service hadn't even started and I'd already decided I didn't like the songs they were going to sing or the leaders who were going to lead them. Can you sense the spiritual arrogance just oozing out of me? I didn't—at least, not yet.

The prideful and stubborn mindset that I had at that moment in Gatlinburg is, sadly, the same mindset many have not just for a moment or two but for their entire lives. As I sat in that church that evening, I obviously considered the newer songs to be better and cooler than the older ones. But for some, it's just the opposite: They feel the older worship songs and styles are superior to the new. Either

way, the thinking remains the same: People tend to assume that their way is the best and perhaps only *true* way to worship.

🐦 Read Revelation 4:6-8. Write what the living creatures say in the last part of verse 8.

The living creatures' song here is very similar to their song of the seraphim in Isaiah 6:3. In fact, put together, those words from the Old and New Testaments could even be two verses of the same song! These living creatures "never stop saying, 'Holy, holy, holy.' " Apparently what we have here is an "old and traditional" song (so to speak). It's the same song they'd been singing way back in Isaiah's time—and which they'll still be singing at the end of the age!

🐦 Now read Revelation 5:8-10. How is this song different from the one shared in Revelation 4:8?

Imagine that. Revelation 4 and 5 record the most powerful worship service in the entire Bible, and includes both old and new music!

It's worth reiterating: Style is *not* the issue with God. He loves all kinds of music—as long as it honors him. What matters to the Lord is not so much what we sing, but how we sing it. God wants to see that our music is flowing from hearts that truly worship him.

Back to that night in rural Gatlinburg…As those song leaders started their first song, I noticed about fifty teenagers lined up in the front rows of the church. My initial thought was, "I really feel sorry for them. There's no way they're going to like this music." But to my surprise, they all picked up hymn books and joined in the singing.

Then something extraordinary happened. As they sang those old songs, several of the young people started lifting their hands in praise, and their voices grew louder and louder. I even noticed a couple of them begin to cry! Their focus wasn't on what kind of music they liked or didn't like—their focus was on the Lord and on giving him praise.

As I watched with amazement those teenagers worshipping God at the top of their lungs, I realized I'd been very wrong and very judgmental. The people in that congregation weren't the ones who needed to learn something about praise and worship. *I was.*

Keep It Real

Take time today or tomorrow to listen to some Christian music you'd never listen to normally. Be sure it's stuff that's not your style. Listen several times. Your goal isn't to like the musical style. Rather, try your best (with God's help!) to worship God through the words of the songs. This is a very important exercise, so make it a priority.

This week's meditation verse is Philippians 2:4. Write it out below. As you do, think about how this verse can help you as you worship with Christians of all kinds and tastes.

JOURNAL

Keep It Pure

Ask God to search your heart right now. When you see someone praising God in a style of music you dislike, do you feel somehow that God isn't as pleased with their worship as he is with yours? If so, why? What's God showing you that you should correct about your opinions? Write down your thoughts.

JOURNAL

It *Is* About Sensitivity

Not long ago I was jogging past a large church. Its beautiful chimes were ringing out the tune of an old hymn. At the same time, on the opposite side of the street, a jacked-up car blaring hip-hop bass beats pulled up to the stoplight. Talk about stereophonic confusion! I didn't know whether I should bust a move or find a quiet place to meditate! As humorous and bizarre as that moment was, it also reminded me that we live in a world full of musical differences and preferences.

As we saw yesterday, any song that honors God and is scripturally accurate is suitable to be sung at church. However, not every song is suitable every time the church gathers. That's because of a thing called *sensitivity*…

While particular musical styles shouldn't be an issue for us, they still need to be considered. We've already seen how the kind of God-honoring music we sing and play doesn't change our relationship with God and how he responds to us. On the other hand, the music we choose to listen to and sing may at times have an adverse effect on the relationships we have with *other people*. And, as we'll learn today, the way we treat each other ultimately affects how we relate to and please our Lord.

Look up John 13:34-35. How do you think this verse might relate to musical choices?

Now, with that in mind, let's consider the following scenarios:

Scenario #1: Joe bought a CD of his favorite kind of music—alternative Christian rock—as a Christmas gift for his girlfriend, Jenny. He told her they could listen to the music when they were together in her car. Problem is, Joe knew that Jenny can't stand rock music—she prefers Bach and Beethoven! Did Joe act lovingly toward Jenny or selfishly and *un*lovingly?

Scenario #2: A youth praise band decided it was time to "show those old people some good music for a change." So on a Sunday night, they performed a modern song that had screaming guitars and loud drums. When the senior adults cringed and placed their fingers over their ears, the youth band didn't turn down the volume—they played even louder. Did the band act lovingly toward those seasoned adults, or were they selfish and *un*loving?

Scenario #3: The young adults of a local congregation asked if some new, more contemporary choruses could be included in the Sunday morning music services. However, the charter members voted it down without even sitting down to talk to the "young folks" and consider their reasons for wanting the change. Did the charter members show love toward the younger people, or were they unloving and self-centered?

Scenario #4: Sarah was asked by a friend to come and sing a solo at her friend's church. The friend explained that the church was more reserved and traditional than most. So, even though Sarah personally preferred singing a more modern song, she selected an older piece she thought the people there would enjoy and relate to more. Did Sarah exemplify a loving and honoring attitude toward that traditional congregation, or did she display a selfish and unloving attitude?

Of all the people we just read about, which one got it? Which one seemed to understand and embrace the principle of sensitivity toward other believers?

Sarah was willing to put aside her personal preferences and agendas and focus instead on ministering to the people she was singing to—and, therefore, she ministered to her Lord.

Why is it that we want to force our music on other believers just because we like it? Who is it we apparently love the most: them or ourselves? Write your thoughts about that here.

JOURNAL

A key passage for this principle of sensitivity toward others is Philippians 2:3-4. Read it now.

Let's expand on this passage a bit, to help drive home our point today. In these verses Paul was clearly referring to *all* the interests a person may have. So no doubt he was talking about musical tastes as well.

You'll notice below that I've left blanks at strategic places. As you read these powerful instructions by Paul, write the word *music* or *musical* into each of the blanks, and then read back through it.

> Let [no] _____ be done through selfish ambition or conceit, but in lowliness of mind let each esteem others better than himself. Let each of you look out not only for his own _____ interests, but also for the _____ interests of others (NEW KING JAMES VERSION).

When we put others and their interests above what we want, we're poised to let the world know we are Christians by our love.

Keep It Real

Read Psalm 27:1-2. Try making up a simple melody, and then sing those verses. Don't be concerned with what style your melody is. Determine instead to simply lift your voice to God. Savor the "taste" of true, biblical worship like David expressed in the words of Psalm 27.

Keep It Pure

Do you sometimes find it hard to worship at church because you don't like the style of music? Search your heart right now. Why *do* you "do worship"? Is your real motive to bless your God, or is it really more about what you like? Think about it: Are you willing to lay aside your own musical tastes and choose instead to worship the Lord with both younger and older Christians—even when it's through a style of music you don't personally prefer? Write your thoughts below.

JOURNAL

It's Even More About Substance

What is it about Christian songs that makes them "Christian"? More specifically, what makes a worship song a worship song? Think about it: More often than not, it isn't the melody or how a song *sounds* that sets it apart. The fact is, you usually can't know for sure whether it's a worship song until you've heard the lyrics.

If you're like a lot of people, you don't think much about the words of a song or what they might be trying to communicate. All you know is you like that song. Maybe your thinking is, "After all, if a song sounds good, what does it matter what the words say?" But if we're going to call certain songs "worship songs," we'd better be sure we know what their words say and mean.

While song lyrics might not be important to us, if they're songs about God, then those lyrics are very important to him. And when it comes to what the lyrics of worship songs should represent about God and the Bible, there's no room to waver based on what people may think and what they like. God's Word is not up for debate or change.

Listen to what the Lord told Joshua: "Only be strong and very courageous, being careful to do according to all the law which Moses my servant commanded you; turn not from it to the right hand or to the left, that you may have good success wherever you go" (Joshua 1:7, REVISED STANDARD VERSION).

Let's look at what Jesus has to say about our worship.

Read what Jesus said to the Samaritan woman about worship in John 4:21-24. What does this mean to you?

JOURNAL

PURE PRAISE
FOR YOUTH

Worship is, first of all, a matter of the *heart*. That's why we learned in Week 1 that the essence of worship is to "love the Lord your God with all your heart and with all your soul and with all your strength" (Deuteronomy 6:5). You might think of it like this: The heart is the fountainhead of our worship, and the worship songs we sing and play should represent the love that's bubbling out from our hearts.

But a pure and passionate heart isn't all that's required for our worship to be acceptable to God. The *focus* of our worship must be on the true and living God—the God who is *Spirit*, the God of the Bible. When our understanding and concept of God become distorted, we're no longer worshipping the true God. Instead, we're worshipping *our* version of God—which, in essence, is a false god. In the same way, when the words of our praise songs don't accurately represent the Lord as he revealed himself in Scripture, then we're not really singing to him, but rather to a "golden calf" of our own making (Exodus 32). Ouch!

There's one more requirement Jesus wants us to see regarding the substance of our worship. Not only must we correctly represent who God *is*, but also what God *says*. Any worship that flows from our lips and our lives must also properly represent God's written Word, the Bible.

When Jesus reprimanded the Pharisees in Matthew 15:1-10, he was basically warning them that God had said one thing, but they were saying something else. They were *misrepresenting* God's Word. Jesus, therefore, called their worship a farce.

They were replacing God's commands with their own man-made laws. They weren't worshipping God in truth, and it is *truth* that must be the *foundation* of all our worship. That's why it's so important to be sure the lyrics in our worship songs are just as correct and accurate before God as our hearts are.

As the people of Judah marched toward their enemies, they sang a powerful worship song. The lyrics were "Praise the Lord, for His mercy endures forever" (2 Chronicles 20:21, NKJV). That simple song is an excellent example of the kind of worship song that both honors and pleases the Lord. Those were words the people of Judah desperately needed and wanted to express to their awesome God. And not only was the song scripturally accurate—describing *what God said*—it also epitomized the very heart of God and *who he is*.

The Father, Son, and Holy Spirit—that's who we worship. That's who we sing to. That's who we sing *about*. And whether we sing the songs, play them, write them, or just ride down the road listening to them, let's be sure they're songs that properly represent the Lord and are worthy to be sung straight to the Father's heart.

Keep It Real

If you have a worship song on your music player or computer, listen to the words right now. You could also sing a worship song that comes to mind. Does the song express who God is and what he's said in his Word? Are the lyrics words your heart longs to say to God? If so, commit to singing and meditating on those words over and over throughout your day as you praise him.

Below, write out this week's meditation verse, Philippians 2:4. Then read it through several times slowly. Try saying it from memory.

JOURNAL

Keep It Pure

Make a quick list of the music you listen to most often. Don't just write down Christian songs. List all the songs you can think of you that you listen to.

JOURNAL

Now, look closely at those songs. Think about the lyrics. Are they songs that feed your spirit and encourage your walk with God? Are they biblically based? Or do the words include ideas and concepts which are foreign—even contrary— to the teachings of the Bible? Take some time now before God to review your song files. What can stay, and what should go?

In your list above, place a check next to songs you feel are wholesome and honoring to God. Then mark an X next to songs you may need to stop listening to.

PURE PRAISE
FOR YOUTH

Today's lesson is not so much about worshipping with others as it is about worshipping *in front of* others.

My sixth-grade son came home from school the other day and said, "Dad, I've started praying over my food at lunch every day." When I asked him how it was going, he said, "All my friends look at me and ask me why I'm bowing my head."

Worshipping God in public requires faith and boldness, for sure. Yet, as a follower of Jesus you're called to "let your light shine before men, that they may see your good deeds and praise your Father in heaven" (Matthew 5:16).

Think about it. If worship is only about telling God we love him, why doesn't he just take us to heaven already? Wouldn't we do a better job of worshipping him there, where we'd see him face to face? Why would God leave Christians on the earth? I believe it's so we can be salt and light to those around us (Matthew 5:13-14). Whether we're at church with other Christ-followers or hanging out with our friends at the mall, we should never be ashamed to lift up praise to God and to talk with others about how good God is.

Naturally, we want our friends and family to worship God with us. And we should hope and pray that they will. But any person who's ever tried to live for Jesus in his or her high school will tell you that some people simply won't follow Christ no matter how much they may see our light shine.

Remember from yesterday what the people of Judah sang as they marched toward their enemies in 2 Chronicles 20? They sang, "Praise the Lord, for His mercy endures forever" (NKJV). By what they said, they clearly *wanted* everyone to worship God. But how effective were they? Did they really influence all those within earshot? Did everyone praise the Lord because of their passionate pleas?

Certainly some did. Many of those soldiers who followed no doubt chose to worship. And it's safe to assume that several spectators who gathered along the route were motivated to join them in praise to their God. However, even though many did decide to worship, the answer to our question is still *no*. They didn't influence everyone. No one will ever have a 100-percent following.

Glow With God

So, if we can't always influence those around us to worship, what *can* we do every time we're in public? What can we accomplish 100 percent of the time we worship our Lord in front of others?

Read 1 Peter 2:9. How does this verse encourage you in worship?

JOURNAL

Do you remember the bold request Moses made of God on Mount Sinai in Exodus 33? He said to the Lord, "Now show me your glory," which God did. When Moses came down from the mountain, what was different about him? It was obvious to all that Moses had been with God because he had "the glow that shows."

In the same way, it should be evident to others that we've been with the Lord. We're supposed to *show forth* God's praises. Now mind you, that doesn't give us an excuse to be "showy" with our worship. It's not about drawing attention to ourselves. We're in the *glow* business, not show business. People need to see us shine for *God.*

People must *want* to come with us to worship the Lord. We can't *force* others into God's presence. But like Moses, we can bring God's presence to *them.* Listen to what Dan DeHaan wrote in his amazing book *The God You Can Know*: "Today we must do the same thing that Moses did. Those of us who are leaders must carry God's presence into the lives of people. Most of us do the opposite. We carry people into the presence of God. We must come down from His presence to minister with anointing from above." [1]

For those of us who help lead worship in a band or choir, how can we know if we've reached our goal of bringing God's presence to those listening? How can *any* worshipper of Jesus be sure we've *illumined* those who happen to be watching us when we praise?

The answer is found in 2 Chronicles 20:29. The nations weren't talking about Judah after their enemies were defeated; they weren't giving the people of Judah the credit. They were talking about the Lord! That's how we know we've illumined those around us—God gets all the praise in the end! The people of Judah proclaimed God's praises, and the world stood up and took notice—not of their great accomplishments, but of God's great power!

For ten years, Brian "Head" Welch played lead guitar for the multi-platinum-selling metal band Korn. Then he met Jesus. On a YouTube video where Brian is getting a tattoo, he describes how he came to know Christ. He visited a church, and in his own words, "I went in there and I saw all these people and they were raising

their hands at the ceiling and I'm like, these people are…weird. Are they stupid or do they got something that I need? I didn't understand it. I went home and I go, 'Jesus, if you're real, make me not want to do drugs anymore.'" [2]

I want you to notice what Brian *saw* when he walked into that church. The first thing he noticed was worshippers raising their hands in praise to their Lord! And God used those people's bold upward worship to help change Brian's life forever.

Keep It Real

Decide today (or tomorrow if you're doing this before going to bed) that you'll talk about God to three people. For example, if someone asks you how you're doing, you might say: "God's good, so life's good" or "God loves me, so I'm doing great!"

Don't worry so much about what your friends may think, and don't try to be funny or cool when you talk about the Lord. Just be yourself and be sincere. It's important that you're genuinely *concerned* for those you meet and talk with.

Keep It Pure

Paul said, "For I am not ashamed of this Good News about Christ. It is the power of God at work, saving everyone who believes" (Romans 1:16, NEW LIVING TRANSLATION). When other people in church are singing and lifting their hands to God, do you tend to hold back because you don't want someone to laugh at you and think you're strange? What about when you're around your friends? Do you tend to keep your praise of God hidden away inside you? Journal an honest prayer to the Lord now. Tell him how you feel at those moments, and ask him to help give you courage not to be ashamed to praise him in public.

JOURNAL

[1] Dan DeHaan, *The God You Can Know* (Chicago, IL: Moody Press, 1982), 35-36.
[2] *Brian "Head" Welch get tattoo in LA Ink* [Video file, 2009]. Retrieved from http://www.youtube.com/watch?v=1WOnoOskWDY

Power to Worship

I once heard a pastor give this humorous illustration: Imagine you're at an automobile dealership shopping for a car. You find one that looks and runs great. So you pay the salesperson the money, and you receive the keys. You climb into your shiny new vehicle and put the keys in the ignition—but you don't crank the engine. Instead, you simply put the shifter in neutral, and then you get out of the car and begin to *push* it out of the parking lot!

Can you imagine the look on the salesperson's face if someone really did that? How silly would it be to strain yourself pushing a brand-new car down the highway? I mean, why would someone have a powerful engine under the hood and not use it? That would be crazy!

So how crazy is it when we as Christians have the King of kings and Lord of lords living inside us, yet we live like we don't? How ridiculous is it when we ignore the awesome power available to us? Because we trust Jesus as our Savior, we have "the Spirit of him who raised Jesus from the dead" dwelling in us (Romans 8:11)! Talk about some power under the hood (and in the heart)!

As you've read this week's lessons on worshipping with and before others, maybe you've thought, That sounds good, but I just don't know if I can do that—especially in front of my friends. Here's a news flash: *You can't.* There's no way any of us can worship and live for God 24/7 on our own. We must allow the Holy Spirit to live his life through us. We simply don't have the strength to do it on our own. Zechariah 4:6 makes this clear: "It is not by force nor by strength, but by my Spirit, says the Lord Almighty" (NLT).

While in college I did a study on the ministry of Jesus in the book of Luke. What I found in chapters 3 and 4 was nothing short of startling, and it forever solidified my reliance on the Holy Spirit as my source of power. I want to walk you through this series of verses now just as I discovered them that particular morning in my dorm room. I really want you to see this for yourself!

Stop now and pray. Ask God to give you insight and an open heart to what he wants to show you today from his Word.

As you go through each of these "discovery" steps, be sure to answer each question before you move to the next one.

Open your Bible and read Luke 3:21-23. Describe the role the Spirit played at Jesus' baptism.

🐦 Now read Luke 4:1-2. Why do you think this verse points out that Jesus is "full of the Holy Spirit"?

🐦 Verses 3-13 describe Jesus' temptation by the devil. Now look at verse 14 very closely. Why do you think Jesus being full of the Holy Spirit is mentioned again here?

🐦 What was the result of Jesus being tempted?

🐦 Now read Luke 4:16-19. Do you think it's important that the Holy Spirit is again mentioned? Why or why not?

Did you catch everything that happened? Let's review:

- Jesus began his ministry the day the *Spirit* descended on him.
- The *Holy Spirit* was controlling Jesus as the *Spirit* led him and filled him.
- The *Spirit's* power was on Jesus, and that caused the news of him to spread.
- The very first public words of Jesus' ministry accredited the *Spirit's* anointing him.

And if that's not enough, check this out: It was not until after the *Spirit* had filled and empowered Jesus that he did his first miracle (John 2:1-11).

Here's what the Lord whispered very loudly to my heart as I sat stunned at my desk that early weekday morning: "Son, if Jesus needed the power of my Spirit, how much more do *you* need the Holy Spirit anointing and helping you every day?"

Ephesians 5:18 says, "Don't be drunk with wine…Instead, be filled with the Spirit." It's not enough to have God's Spirit living in you and me just because we know Jesus; we must continue to be filled with him every day. Every day that is not a Spirit-filled day is a wasted day. It's worth saying again: To worship God, we *must* be filled with his Spirit.

Keep It Real

Tune up your vocal chords and sing a praise song to God right now. Don't just hum it. Let the melody you're making in your heart come out of you like a fountain of flowing water! Come on, you sing in the shower, right? So sing to the Lord right where you are! Remember, God loves to hear you sing! He should—he made your voice!

Write this week's meditation verse, Philippians 2:4, below. Do it from memory if possible.

JOURNAL

To be filled with the Holy Spirit, you need to get *un*-full of yourself. Here are a few simple steps to help you: (1) Completely surrender every room and closet of your heart's home. It's been said, "If he's not Lord of all, he's not Lord *at* all." (2) Invite the Spirit to come and fill you up with only him. (3) To keep being filled, claim the Spirit's filling daily, and continually surrender afresh to his voice and direction.

Take some time now to pray. Tell God you give yourself completely to him today. Then thank him for filling you with his Spirit.

JOURNAL WEEK 5 | DAY 5

For this session, you'll need:

- CD or MP3 player
- Worship music on CD or MP3; you'll need to play two tracks—one at the beginning of your gathering and one at the end

Leader: Select worship music that goes against the style of music your group members prefer. Challenge your group to recognize the God-honoring lyrics in a musical genre they might not select on their own.

GET CONNECTED (15 minutes)

We're going to do something a little different as we begin our time together today. Sit back and relax as I play some music for you—it's some worship music that I *know* you'll enjoy. Pay special attention to the song's lyrics.

Begin playing the song on your CD or MP3 player. If you've chosen a truly challenging song, your students may laugh or groan or make comments; encourage them to remain quiet until the end of the song. Then discuss: → →1

You have your own preferences in worship music—and other people have their own preferred styles that are completely different from yours. But what's important is whether the music honors God and draws us closer to him. Ultimately, substance matters more than the style.

DIG DEEPER (20 minutes)

Discuss together: → →2

Form groups of three. Have a volunteer read Philippians 2:1-4, and then take ten minutes to discuss these questions → →3

Bring everyone back together after 10 minutes. Share highlights and insights from your discussion time.

→ → **1**
- Did you enjoy the music you just listened to, dislike it, or are you unsure? Is your response more about the *style* of the music or the *words* of the song?
- What message did the words communicate to you? How much, if at all, did the style of the song get in the way of the message? Explain.
- How have you struggled with the style of worship or music—or other "style" issues—at church?

→ → **2**
- How would *you* define what Dwayne calls "spiritual arrogance"? Give examples if you can.

- What are some of the dangers in believing that your way of worshipping God is better than the way other Christians worship God?

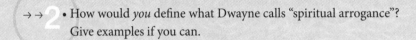
PHILIPPIANS 2:1-4

→ → **3**
- What's the connection between putting others above yourself and pursuing a lifestyle of worship? Why does God want us to be so deeply concerned about other people?

- Besides being sensitive to musical differences, how can we place other Christians higher than ourselves?

BRING IT TO LIFE (20 minutes)

As we pursue a lifestyle of worship, it's important to remember that God is the one who creates lasting change in our lives. We make choices that point us in the direction God desires, and we have the responsibility of obeying God. But God is the one who produces spiritual change within us.

Read Zechariah 4:6, and then discuss these questions: → → 4

We're going to close our time together with another worship song—and just like our opening song, this may not be your preferred style of music. But once again, listen to the words and allow them to speak to you as we worship God together.

After the song, pray for your group, asking that God would give each of you a greater appreciation for how each Christian is able to worship in a uniquely meaningful way.

ZECHARIAH 4:6

→ → **4** • In this week's readings, Dwayne wrote, "There's no way any of us can worship and live for God 24/7 on our own. We must allow the Holy Spirit to live his life through us. We simply don't have the strength to do it on our own." How do those words challenge you?

• What are some specific ways you can trust God's power through the Holy Spirit in your life this coming week?

DAY 1

Worship That Ministers

JOURNAL

Let's jump right into this final week.

Mark 12:30 describes the essence of true worship to God, "Love the Lord your God with all your heart and with all your soul and with all your mind and with all your strength." 🐦 Take a moment and think about this: How is loving God the same as worshipping him?

If we love God with everything we are, in effect we're telling him, "God, you're more important to me than anything else in life. You're worthy of all my love and adoration. I worship you alone."

But it's not enough just to claim we love God. We must show it by the things we do and say. There's a story in Luke about a woman who worshipped Jesus through her bold actions. 🐦 Read Luke 7:36-47. Notice how the woman demonstrated her love for Jesus in verses 37-38. How do you think her extravagant worship made Jesus feel? How would *you* feel if someone showed you such selfless love?

From what Jesus said to Simon the Pharisee in verses 44-47, I think it's safe to say he was encouraged and helped through the love the woman showed to Jesus. Another word for her act of worship is *ministry*. She *ministered* to Jesus when she anointed him with oil.

There are many ways you and I can minister to Jesus through our love and worship of him. Every time we do one of these, we bless him. I've listed several ideas on the next page. Can you think of any others to add to the list?

PURE PRAISE
FOR YOUTH

Ways to Minister to Jesus:

> Obey him.
> Tell him I love him.
> Trust him no matter what.
> Do something bold that brings honor to God.
> Tell others about him.
> Do my best in school.
> Obey my parents.
> Read God's Word.

_____

_____

_____

Now, you just read in Mark 12:30 that loving God is the most important commandment. But actually, you saw only half of that commandment. Jesus wasn't done yet. What he goes on to say in verse 31 is surprising. He says, "The second is equally important: 'Love your neighbor as yourself.'"

Did you catch that? Jesus said that loving others is as important as loving God! And to make sure he got his point across, he immediately followed his two-part statement with this clincher: "There is no greater commandment than these." Notice that the word *commandment* is singular. Loving God and loving others is really *one* commandment, not two separate ideas.

So what does that mean? What should it teach us? It means we can't truly love God if we don't also love other people, and vice versa. Just as we must *show* our love to God through our actions, we must also willingly and generously show our love to others by how we treat them and *minister* to their needs.

Being a Minister

If you're like a lot of people, when you hear the word *minister*, the first person you think of is your pastor or someone who works at your church. But ministry is not just for preachers and people who get paid to do it. Ministering to others means encouraging and helping them—and that's something every Christian is called to do every day.

You shouldn't only see yourself as a minister when you help an elderly couple with their yardwork or go on a mission trip with your youth group. Ministry is more than something you do every once in a while when it's convenient and you're in the mood. You are called by God to be a minister *all the time*.

Another word for ministry is *serving*. Listen to what Peter said: "Each one should use whatever gift he has received to serve others, faithfully administering God's grace in its various forms. If anyone speaks, he should do it as one speaking the very words of God. If anyone serves, he should do it with the strength God provides, so that in all things God may be praised through Jesus Christ" (1 Peter 4:10-11). When you serve others through God's power, *God* is praised. You worship God by bringing honor to him. What's more, when you minister to others, you're ministering to Jesus himself (Matthew 25:40).

Being a servant isn't glamorous. It often means doing things that are uncomfortable and unpopular. Sometimes serving others can be downright messy and dirty. Yet God must smile when you and I gladly yield ourselves (and *see* ourselves) as *his servants*—nothing more and nothing less.

Keep It Real

This week's meditation passage is Psalm 63:3-4. Write it below. As you write, think about why praising God is a great way to serve him.

JOURNAL

Sing a worship song to the Lord right now. Praise him joyfully for his absolute power and presence in your life today.

Keep It Pure

Read Philippians 2:5-11. Notice how *Jesus the exalted* humbled himself and became *Jesus the servant*. Verse 5 says you must have the same attitude he had.

How do you feel about serving others and putting their needs above your own? Is there someone you know you should try to encourage and help, but you've been putting off or ignoring that person? Have you avoided jumping in to help because you may have to get your hands dirty?

Confess your attitude to God. Ask him to cleanse you and help you to be his servant at all times. Journal your prayer.

JOURNAL

PURE PRAISE
FOR YOUTH

I want you to start today's lesson by repeating this statement after me. Say it out loud: "He is God. I am not." Now say it again—this time with more conviction and volume: "He is God. I am not."

You just acknowledged one of the most foundational truths about worship: If you worship God, you can't worship yourself. Your priority can't be to lift *your* name up. Rather, you must lift the name of Jesus high above your own. You must willingly say what John said: "He must become greater; I must become less" (John 3:30).

John's goal of decreasing in fame so Jesus' fame could increase wouldn't go over well with many people today. Most of us like the idea of being well known. In fact, according to a few recent studies, 51 percent of teenagers say one of their most important goals in life is to become famous.[1] What's more, 31 percent expect they *will* be famous one day.[2] No doubt this thinking is encouraged by reality TV and the Internet, where it seems almost anybody can go viral overnight.

Fame is not necessarily bad; I can think of several famous people who have used their celebrity status as an opportunity to share with others the love of Jesus. Still, the vast majority of people don't see fame as a platform to proclaim the gospel. Rather, they see it mostly as a means to personal happiness and success.

As followers of Jesus, we're not to make happiness and success our goal. Our desire should first be to make the *Lord* famous throughout the earth. Like David, we should "publish his glorious deeds among the nations. Tell everyone about the amazing things he does" (Psalm 96:3, NEW LIVING TRANSLATION). After all, *he's* the Savior, the healer, the forgiver of sins, and the life-changing God. There's nothing we have to offer this lost and hurting world apart from Jesus Christ. He is "the way and the truth and the life" (John 14:6).

All this talk about becoming less so Jesus can become greater is good and important. But let's face it: It's easier said than done. It's one thing to *say* God is God and you're not; it's another to live like you *believe* it. It's one thing to *say* you don't seek credit and recognition, but it's quite another to really *mean* it. It requires something rarely found these days—even among Christians—humility.

Read 1 Peter 5:5-6. Notice verse 6 gives a condition, followed by a promised result. Write that condition and its result in your own words.

First Peter 5:6 contains a powerful and unchangeable spiritual law. When we humble ourselves before God's mighty hand, he will lift us up in due time. Here's a good way to think of it: The law of gravity states that what goes up must come down. The law of divine elevation, on the other hand, states that what comes down through humility will go up through God's exaltation!

Benefits of Humility

With real humility comes true greatness. You see, God wants to elevate you and cause you to shine so others can see *God's* glory through your life. Think about the estimated one sextillion (or 10^{22}) or more stars in the universe.[3] God created each and every one of them. He placed them exactly where he wanted them to be. Those stars had nothing to do with their creation or their location. They have no say over how much they shine. Yet, each one plays a magnificent and distinctive role in God's universe.

Like those stars, you were created for God's glory. He designed you to be "children of God without fault in a crooked and depraved generation, in which you shine like stars in the universe" (Philippians 2:15). There's no greater satisfaction than knowing you're fulfilling the purpose for which the Creator made you. You might say that true humility comes with a huge tag that reads Complete Satisfaction Guaranteed!

There's nothing more comforting than knowing that *God* is the one who's lifted you to where you are. Such knowledge takes away the stress of feeling like you have to fight to maintain your position. As Paul said, "If God is for us, who can be against us?" (Romans 8:31b). So humility not only brings satisfaction, it can also give a sense of security.

And if that's not enough, here's yet another benefit: Being humble can bring you serenity. I Peter 5:6 says "in due time" God will exalt you. God has a plan; your every step has already been determined by him. He'll raise you up when and how he sees fit. That should give you tremendous peace of mind.

There was a time in my life years ago when I really wanted to be a Christian music artist. I can see now how that wasn't God's plan for my life, but at the time it seemed the best way for me to use my talents and passions to glorify God. I remember buying a CD about how to "get discovered" in the Christian music industry. It was full of ideas. One suggestion was to go and "camp out" at the doorsteps of some of the record labels!

The advice that helped me most, though, wasn't about what I *could* do, but more about what I *shouldn't* do. One of the artists on the CD said that Christians shouldn't focus so much on promoting themselves to others. Rather, we should first go *deep* in our relationship with God. The artist said that we should "knock on heaven's door (through prayer) before we knock on people's doors."

Then he quoted a passage from the Psalms that I'd never noticed before: "For not from the east or from the west and not from the wilderness comes lifting up; but it is God who executes judgment, putting down one and lifting up another" (Psalm 75:6-7, REVISED STANDARD VERSION).

What I learned from those amazing verses—and what I pray you discover—is this: You can *trust* God to open doors of opportunity both *when* and *where* he wants you to enter. You don't have to fret about the future. It doesn't really matter whether you're ever elevated to fame and fortune. That's God's business. You can be at peace simply knowing you're in God's will at this moment. You can enjoy life today right where God has placed you. And you can shine like a star for the Lord, as you worship him and humbly minister to those around you.

There's one more incredible benefit to humility we dare not miss: God's *grace*. 1 Peter 5:5 includes these words: "God opposes the proud but gives grace to the humble." What an awesome promise! You and I desperately need his unmerited favor on our lives each and every day. His grace is always enough to see us through every opportunity and every trial of life.

Keep It Real

Take time now to boldly thank and praise God. Use at least two of the eight expressions of praise you learned about in Week 2—sing, shout, clap, kneel, dance, testify, play an instrument, and raise holy hands.

You may be tempted to skip over this exercise, but do it anyway—even if you don't think you have time or don't really want to do it. Remember, God desires and *deserves* your praise!

Keep It Pure

True success isn't defined by others' applause. Jesus says, "He who is least among you all—he is the greatest" (Luke 9:48). You and I will never be bigger in God's eyes than when we're ordinary servants…of the most high King!

Search your heart now. Ask the Lord to reveal any prideful motives and actions. Do you think you're too good to perform certain tasks for others? Pray that God will form a servant's heart in you that's humble and ready to do whatever's needed.

---

[1] Sharon Jayson (2007). *Generation Y's goal? Wealth and fame.* Retrieved from USA Today website: http://www.usatoday.com/news/nation/2007-01-09-gen-y-cover_x.htm

[2] Jake Halpern (2010). Press release for *Fame Junkies.* Retrieved from Houghton Mifflin Harcourt website: http://www.hmhbooks.com/booksellers/press_release/fame/

[3] Fraser Cain (2009). *How Many Stars?* Retrieved from Universe Today website: http://www.universetoday.com/24328/how-many-stars/

Worshippers for Life

The greatest statement we can ever hope to hear is our heavenly Father saying to us, "Well done, good and faithful servant" (Matthew 25:21). When I was in college, I remember writing in my journal this goal for my life: To say as Paul said, "I have fought the good fight, I have finished the race, and I have remained faithful' " (2 Timothy 4:7, NLT). Even now when I read those words, I'm challenged to be all I can be for my Lord and to never stop worshipping him. I really want to hear God say "well done" to me one day.

There are so many who seem on fire for God for a few weeks or a few months, but then they cool down. Their enthusiasm and commitment to God fades; they stop worshipping the Lord and living for him. What God desires and deserves are worshippers who serve him all their lives, who never stop growing and glowing for Jesus. For that very reason, during these final three lessons, I want to help teach you how to be a *lifelong worshipper*, serving God for the rest of your life.

Paul's highest goal in life was to complete the mission God had given him on earth. And he accomplished that mission. Paul wrote 2 Timothy in a dungeon cell near the end of his life. It was the last letter he would ever write. As he reviewed his own life-goals in 2 Timothy 4:7, Paul was also letting Timothy in on some principles which are necessary for any of us to finish well.

Keep Fighting

The principle for finishing well that we'll look at today is to *keep fighting*. Paul said, "I have fought the good fight." Anyone who follows Jesus needs to recognize that the Christian life is not a playground; it's a battlefield, where conflicts are won and lost in real spiritual battles.

Of course, the enemies Christians are battling are not other people, especially not other followers of Jesus (although it may seem that way at times!). Nothing good will come from waging war against each other in the family of God. The "good fight" Paul had fought was "against evil rulers and authorities of the unseen world, against mighty powers in this dark world, and against evil spirits in the heavenly places" (Ephesians 6:12b, NLT).

Satan is determined to destroy God's people. And on your own, you're no match for the powers of darkness. When John wrote, "Greater is he that is in you, than he that is in the world" (1 John 4:4, KING JAMES VERSION), he was implying that without Christ, we are *less* powerful than the devil.

According to Ephesians 2:2-3, the "prince of the power of the air" (KJV) is not the only source of your temptations. Your fleshly nature and the world around you can also tempt you to go astray. In order to overcome temptation,

you have to *flee* it when it comes along, and have *faith* in God and his promises. Don't just say "no" to temptation—say "yes" to God.

The Weapons of Our Warfare

No matter how much you may guard against it, you'll still be tempted at times. Rogue thoughts may bombard your mind when you least expect them. "Your enemy the devil prowls around like a roaring lion looking for someone to devour" (1 Peter 5:8). For that reason, you need to have weapons ready to use against him.

In Ephesians 6 Paul described the "whole armor of God" needed to "stand against the wiles of the devil" (verse 11, KJV). He listed several necessary pieces in that passage. Read Ephesians 6:10-18 now. Why do we need so much armor?

JOURNAL

Read back through the list of armor. Notice that all of the armor pieces are used for defense—except one. The Word of God, the *Bible*, is the Spirit's sword to utterly defeat the enemy.

Remember what Jesus did every time he was tempted by the devil in the wilderness? He quoted Scripture (Luke 4:1-12). That's why it's absolutely essential that you hide God's Word in your heart. Like Jesus, you can recall it the very moment you're tempted, to keep you from sinning against God (Psalm 119:11).

Another effective weapon is expressive, heartfelt praise. In 2 Chronicles 20, the people of Judah didn't have swords and spears as they marched toward their enemies. Instead, they boldly lifted up praise to God for all to see and hear. Verse 22 describes what happened: "As they began to sing and praise, the Lord set ambushes against the men of Ammon and Moab and Mount Seir who were invading Judah, and they were defeated." Their praise was effective because it was based on the truth of Scripture.

When your praise is based on what the Bible says, it frustrates and confuses the devil and his demons. So the next time you're tempted to get discouraged or frightened or rebellious, turn your eyes and thoughts upward toward heaven. Quote Scripture and fervently praise God from your surrendered heart. Then watch what happens as your (invisible) enemies scurry away in horror and defeat!

Keep fighting the good fight!

If you're physically able, stand up right now where you are. Do a dance of praise before the Lord. Your body will hate you for it, but your spirit will be reminded it's not about you and your flesh. It's about showing how much you love your Lord! Go ahead. You'll never be in "the mood." Just make this "sacrifice" of praise anyway!

Review this week's meditation passage, Psalm 63:3-4. Write it below as a prayer to God.

JOURNAL

James 4:7 says, "Submit yourselves, then, to God. Resist the devil, and he will flee from you." Have you submitted every area of yourself to God? If not, you can't fight Satan and win; he'll spear you through that place in your armor you've left unprotected.

Pray and surrender your will and mind to the Lord right now. Ask God to help you love him more deeply in the days and months ahead. Journal your prayer below.

JOURNAL

My boys have me hooked on one of their new video games. The object is to see how long you can stay alive against a bunch of dead guys coming at you! (It may not sound like fun, but trust me, it is.) I've noticed something very important to one's survival in this game: You have to stay completely zoned in to what you're doing! You can't take your eyes off the screen or your hands off the controller for even a second, or you're history. And the higher up you go in levels of play, the more focused you have to stay!

It's that way in the Christian life, too. If you're going to finish well, you have to stay alert and determined to win. You have to be careful not to take yourself out of the game, so to speak, through careless mistakes and poor judgment.

Paul was up for that challenge. He saw his entire life as a race he didn't intend to lose. And near the end of his life he told Timothy: "I have finished the race" (2 Timothy 4:7). Paul's mission was to impact as many as he could with the gospel of Christ. He knew what a devastating blow would be dealt to that mission if he didn't live out what he preached. Understanding his passion to finish well, it's no wonder he was so determined to keep focused.

Read the following passage, really try to absorb it, and write your impressions afterward: "But one thing I do: Forgetting what is behind and straining toward what is ahead, I press on toward the goal to win the prize for which God has called me heavenward in Christ Jesus" (Philippians 3:13b-14).

JOURNAL

Paul's prize was far greater than anything this earth has to offer. His was an incorruptible, heavenly prize—the "upward call of God in Christ" (Philippians 3:14, New King James Version). The thought of hearing God say "well done" motivated him—and should motivate any Christian—to keep on moving forward.

Peter said, "*Always be prepared* to give an answer to everyone who asks you to give the reason for the hope that you have" (1 Peter 3:15, italics added). But let's face it, having to be "on your game" day in and day out and week after week, staying consistent in your walk with Jesus, can get really challenging after a while. Sometimes just having a daily quiet time seems like hard work!

That's why we must heed the instructions of Hebrews 12:1-2. This is a powerful and practical passage that shows how to stay focused for the long haul.

Read that passage now. According to these verses, what are some things you should do to help you live for God each day? What would that look like to you?

Some Pointers for Focusing

Hebrews 12:1 says, "throw off everything that hinders and the sin that so easily entangles." *Deal with distractions* that will draw your attention off your goals, slow you down, and discourage you. Satan has a whole bag full of tricks to distract and ensnare you. It might even be an activity you're involved with that seems harmless or even helpful, yet it's not God's will for you. Or it may be a pet sin that only you and God know about. *Any* sin must be confessed and stopped. Continuing in sin will eat away at you and destroy you like a cancer.

Discipline is required to keep you focused. Like the story of the tortoise and the hare, the turtle may not have been faster than the rabbit, but he set his pace and won the race. Anybody can have a great start, but seasoned runners know how to stay energized for the tall hills and long stretches ahead. While others are off having "fun," seasoned runners stay focused and finish in first place.

When it comes to focusing, *direction* is obviously also pretty important. It helps to know which way you're supposed to go! Colossians 3:2 says, "Think about the things of heaven, not the things of earth" (NLT). The chorus to an old hymn tells exactly where you and I should focus our attention—and why:

> *Turn your eyes upon Jesus.*
> *Look full in his wonderful face.*
> *And the things of earth will grow strangely dim*
> *In the light of his glory and grace.*

In order to keep "your eyes upon Jesus" day in and day out, you must have his *divine power* helping you. *You* are not the one who'll finish your faith. Ultimately, it's not up to *you* to keep yourself in God's family. That's God's job. According to

Hebrews 12:2, Jesus is both the "author and perfecter" of your faith. He started this good work in you when you trusted him as your Savior—and he alone will complete it.

Don't try to live the Christian life on your own. You were never meant to! You have his awesome power—the same power that raised Jesus from the dead—alive inside *you*! Trust the one "who is able to keep you from falling and to present you before his glorious presence without fault and with great joy" (Jude 1:24).

To stay focused, you've also got to have a lot of *determination* along the way. For some, that may mean spending less time on Facebook or in front of the Xbox and more time in the Bible and in prayer. For others, it may mean not hanging out with certain people at school who could pull your focus away from Jesus. It might even mean you'll have to stop dating someone for whom you care deeply, because that person doesn't honor and love the Lord like you do.

Luke 9:51 says, "As the time approached for him to be taken up to heaven, Jesus resolutely set out for Jerusalem." In other words, he was *determined* to stay focused on his mission. That mission was to die for your sins and mine, so we could join him in heaven one day. He *endured* the cross, along with all its shame and persecution.

Here's a sobering thought: Since Jesus was so focused on dying for us, shouldn't we want to *live* for him—no matter what?

Keep It Real

Look back over the pointers for focusing that you just read—dealing with distractions, finding direction, having discipline, trusting his divine power, and having determination. Which do you feel you're strongest in? Which do you need the most help with? Why those particular ones? Write your thoughts below.

{ JOURNAL

Say this week's meditation verses, Psalm 63:3-4, from memory if possible. If not, read them several times until you can begin to quote them.

One of the things I like the most about the video game I've been playing is how you can "respawn." If you get knocked down, you have the opportunity to get right back in the game. That means a *lot* to guys like me who don't play very well!

No matter how determined we are to live for Jesus, we're still going to blow it sometimes. We're going to fail. Like someone said, "The only thing I know I'll do consistently is be *in*consistent." That's why I'm glad 1 John 1:9 promises, "If we confess our sins, he is faithful and just and will forgive us our sins and purify us from all unrighteousness."

Take time now to confess any sins to God. Admit your weaknesses and failures. Thank the Lord for forgiving you and ask him to live his life through you.

JOURNAL

Both my sons trusted Jesus as their Savior when they were in elementary school. One of the first things I did was get out the *New Foxe's Book of Martyrs* and read some stories from it to them. If you're not familiar with that book, it recounts—in graphic detail—the persecutions and deaths of numerous Christians through the centuries.

One particular story I remember us reading together was about a fifteen-year-old in Indonesia named Roy. He was threatened by an angry mob that had burst into the Bible camp where he lived. When they told him he must become a Muslim, Roy replied in a quivering voice, "I am a soldier for Christ." Then an enraged Muslim ripped his stomach open with a knife. Just before he died, Roy said one final word: "Jesus." [1]

How long ago did that happen, you might ask? It was only a few years ago when Roy died for his faith.

You might wonder why I would tell such harrowing and gruesome stories to my children at such young ages. Simply this: I wanted to them to learn, as early as possible, what it might require for them to take a stand for Jesus. I wanted them to count the cost—to understand the dangers and seriousness of calling themselves Christians. One thing's for sure: If they live long enough, my sons will face some hardships and ridicule—as will every man, woman, boy, and girl who wears the name of Jesus and lives openly for him.

Read John 16:33. Why did Jesus say we can take heart and be cheerful regardless of what happens to us? What's your response to this?

JOURNAL

Jesus didn't soft-sell Christianity. He never said it would be easy to be one of his followers. He put it out there and made it very plain: Expect trouble in this world. It's inevitable. The world hated Jesus—why should you expect any better treatment?

I've never had my life threatened or experienced the kind of torture that many Christians have endured. But there was a time in middle school when I got a small taste of what persecution feels like. I'd just committed my life to Jesus during the summer before my sixth-grade year, so when I started school that fall I was determined to live for God. I stopped laughing at dirty jokes. I started taking my Bible to school. And when people used God's name in vain, sometimes I'd ask them to please stop because they were cursing the One I loved. I was far from perfect, mind you, but I was *trying* to worship God with my life and be a witness to others.

My "friends" didn't like my sudden seriousness about being a Christian, so for the next two years they made my life miserable. Lots of times they'd follow close behind me, stepping on my heels, trying to get me to say something bad. On several occasions they backed me up against a wall and berated me with hard questions about God, trying to confuse me and make me mad. I remember many times having to eat alone at lunch because I wasn't cool enough.

One of the things that really helped get me through those tough couple of years was reading about the Apostle Paul. He certainly experienced his share of trouble and persecution during his ministry. Yet in the closing words of his final letter to Timothy, Paul wrote, "I have remained faithful" (2 Timothy 4:7, NLT)—or as *The Message* puts it: "I've…believed all the way." Throughout the centuries people like Paul and fifteen-year-old Roy have "believed all the way" to their final breath.

Nailing It Down

The fact that you've gotten this far in this study says a lot. You obviously have some tenacity and determination about you, and I commend you for that. It takes a lot of discipline to carve out time every day as you have, to invest time with God in his Word.

But now I want to challenge you to something much bigger than a six-week Bible study. I want you to decide right here and now that you're going to be a worshipper for *life*. Decide that from this moment on until your final breath, you're going to praise your God no matter what comes your way.

Tall order, you say? Yes, it is. But you need to nail this down in your mind and heart. Don't put it off any longer. This is it.

Go to a mirror right now and look yourself in the eye. Call yourself by name and say, "You're going to serve God for the rest of your life. You're going to praise him and love him until you die." Let that powerful decision settle into your soul.

Three Things to Keep in Mind

To close our study together, I want to give you three awesome truths that will help you accomplish your radical goal of worshipping the Lord for life.

1. Life is short. Psalm 90:12 says, "Teach us to number our days, that we may gain a heart of wisdom" (NKJV). Even though you're young, you really don't have time to waste. Time moves faster than you think. So make the most of every day you have.

Earlier in Psalm 90, David gave us a formula for "counting our days." In verse 4, he wrote, "For you, a thousand years are as a passing day, as brief as a few night hours" (NLT). Think about it: If a thousand years is like a twelve-hour day to the Lord, then how long are our *lives* from God's perspective? Catch this: If a person lives to be seventy-five years old, he or she's still only *fifty-four minutes* old to God! That's less than an hour! David was trying to drive home the point here that our lives are very, very short—no matter how long we may live on this earth!

What about you? How old are you (in minutes) to God? To find out, simply multiply your age by 0.72. Go ahead—give it a try. You'll be amazed!

2. Judgment is sure. King Solomon had some incredibly wise advice for those your age. He said, "Young people, it's wonderful to be young! Enjoy every minute of it. Do everything you want to do; take it all in. But remember that you must give an account to God for everything you do" (Ecclesiastes 11:9, NLT). It doesn't get much plainer than that. You'd *better* stay faithful, because you're *going* to stand before God one day.

3. God's grace is sufficient. I saved the best truth for last! Lest you think more highly of me than you should, let me set the record straight: I'm a wimp! Apart from God, there's no way I could have ever stood my ground when my "friends" were ridiculing me and giving me such a hard time. God was with me every moment, and he's the one who strengthened me and lived through me. It was only by his grace!

God's undeserved favor is more than able to see you through anything you'll ever face. Years ago I heard someone say, "The will of God will never lead you where the grace of God cannot keep you." I'm living proof of that—and you will be, too! Trust God to hold tight to you through the good times and the bad. God loves you more than you'll ever know.

What great reasons you have to *keep on praising God!*

Quote Psalm 63:3-4 from memory if possible. Say it as a prayer of praise to God.

Then keep it going! Think again about the eight ways to praise you tried out earlier this week, and use some of those right now to have an awesome praise time before God! Thank God for helping you finish this study and for all he's taught you.

JOURNAL

PURE PRAISE
FOR YOUTH

Take some time now to look back over the things you've journaled throughout this study. What's God shown you that you *need* to be sure to remember and apply?

Write a prayer to God asking him to help you worship him for the rest of your life. And may God continue to bless you as you seek to live your prayer out!

[1] John Foxe and Harold J. Chadwick, *New Foxe's Book of Martyrs* (New Brunswick, NJ: Bridge-Logos Publishers, 2001), 376, 377.

For this session, you'll need:

- Several unfolded cardboard boxes (cereal boxes work well!)
- Scissors
- Permanent markers

GET CONNECTED (15 minutes)

Congratulations! We've made it to our final session! So let's jump right in. Form groups of three.

Distribute supplies to each group. Ask each person to cut a piece of cardboard to resemble a tombstone. Allow for variation and creativity in the shapes and sizes of the tombstones.

Now that you've carved your tombstones, it's time to inscribe them. Write a list of words that describe you, a statement you'd like people to say if they thought about your life, or your favorite verse from the Bible—*something* that reflects who you are or how you'd like to be remembered. Once you're finished, share your inscriptions with one another, and tell a little bit about why you chose what you wrote. Then read Matthew 25:14-28, and discuss these questions together: → →1

Give groups ten minutes to discuss, and then regain everyone's attention, keeping them with their groups. Ask for volunteers from each group to share highlights and insights from their discussion time.

Becoming a good and faithful servant of Jesus is something we all can achieve. It doesn't come easily, but as we worship God through our service to him and others, we find that our attitudes shift. We become less self-centered and more Jesus-centered. That's the evidence that we're truly leading a lifestyle of worship.

PURE PRAISE
FOR YOUTH

MATTHEW 25:14-28

→ → **1** • What do you think it means to be a "good and faithful servant" of Jesus?

• Think of someone you know whose tombstone could include the phrase "good and faithful servant of Jesus." Why did that person come to mind?

DIG DEEPER (25 minutes)

Discuss together: → → 2

When we read through the Gospels, we discover how Jesus loved the people around him—and how many of those people deeply loved him back.

Turn back to your groups. (Pause.) Read Luke 7:36-47, and then take ten minutes to discuss these questions: → → 3

Bring everyone back together after ten minutes. Share highlights and insights from your discussion time, particularly regarding the last question.

This week's meditation verses are Psalm 63:3-4. Can I get a volunteer to read those verses for us? → → 4

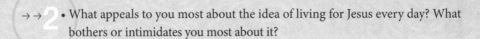

→ → **2** • What appeals to you most about the idea of living for Jesus every day? What bothers or intimidates you most about it?

• Why do you think so many Christians say they love God yet find it difficult to live out their faith? And if it's so difficult, why do you think they even *say* it?

 LUKE 7:36-47

→ → **3** • When have you seen the kind of connection shown here—where Jesus' forgiveness created a deeper love in the person receiving it?

• Do you find it easier to love God or love other people? Why?

• Why can't we truly do one without the other?

 PSALM 63:3-4

→ → **4** • What do you think David meant when he wrote that God's unfailing love was better than life itself? How easy or difficult is it for you to experience what David meant? Why?

BRING IT TO LIFE (20 minutes)

Read 1 Peter 5:5-6, and then discuss these questions: → → 5

Find a partner—ideally, someone who wasn't part of your group earlier. Together, take five minutes to discuss these questions. I'll close us in prayer afterward. → → 6

After five minutes, regain everyone's attention for a closing prayer.

God, thanks for the growth we've experienced through this study. Help us continue growing as worshippers. We want our lives to point others to you so they can experience your love, grace, and forgiveness just as we have experienced these incredible gifts. Help us become people who truly lead lifestyles of worship. We ask this in Jesus' name, amen.

1 PETER 5:5-6

→ → 5 • How appealing is humility to you, really? Explain your answer.

• How is a humble attitude contrary to the attitudes encouraged by our culture? Give examples.

→ → 6 • What comes to mind when you think about the idea of being a "worshipper for life"? What steps can you take in the coming week to put yourself or keep yourself on that path?

• How can we challenge each other to keep pursuing a lifestyle of worship after this study ends?

Invite Mark Hall & Dwayne Moore to help you experience

PURE PRAISE FOR YOUTH

Weekly Teaching Videos

Want to make the most of your time in *Pure Praise for Youth*? Then imagine Mark Hall, lead singer of Casting Crowns, talking with you every week about what you're learning!

Author Dwayne Moore has teamed up with Mark Hall to do weekly teaching videos which highlight the material and will encourage you to keep faithful to the daily devotions in the book.

Got a youth group going through *Pure Praise*? These 10-minute video sessions work really well to enhance your weekly small-group sessions!

What's more, bonus teaching videos are also available which are designed especially for praise bands, to help them understand how and why they lead worship!

Videos are available as digital downloads, or as a complete set on DVD. available at NextLevelWorship.com/store.

NEXT LEVEL WORSHIP
A Next Level Worship Resource